Crazy Quilts
by Machine

J. Marsha Michler

Published by
Krause Publications
700 East State St., Iola, WI 54990-0001
Telephone (715) 445-2214
www.krause.com

Please call or write for our free catalog of publications. Our toll-free number to place an order or obtain a free catalog is 800-258-0929 or please use our regular business telephone 715-445-2214 for editorial comment and further information.

Permission to photocopy patterns for personal use **only** is granted by the author and publisher.

Library of Congress Catalog Number 99-69480
ISBN 0-87341-827-1

Some products in this book are registered trademarks of their respective companies:
Facets™ (Kreinik Mfg. Co. Inc.)
Sulky™ (Sulky of America)
DMC™ (DMC Corporation)
Pearl Crown Rayon®, YLI Select Thread™, and YLI 100% Cotton Quilting Thread™ (YLI)

All photography and illustrations by J. Marsha Michler

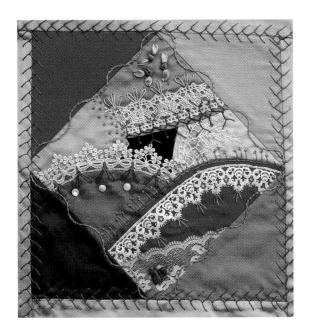

Dedication

This book is dedicated to the memory of my father, RRM, whose ability to revel in the roots of design and the details of construction will keep me wondering forever.

Acknowledgments

Many thanks to my agent Sandy Taylor, editor Amy Tincher-Durik, cover designer Kim Schierl, and book designer Jan Wojtech for their excellent assistance and expertise. For the wonderful supplies, my grateful thanks to Dena Lenham of Kreinik Co. Inc., Vicki Smith of YLI Corporation, Diana Dickey of Artemis, Maggie Backman of Things Japanese, and to Ron Prevoir for the linens. A special "hi" to the members of The Crazy Quilt Benevolent Society and Quiltropolis' CrazyQuilt email list, The Pot O' Gold Investment Club, Tim my dancin' buddy, Margie, Anna, and David, and thanks to my sister for the warm socks. And, last but not least, my thanks to Paul to whom I am ever grateful for assistance with photography and props.

Among the threads used in this book are:

• Kreinik metallics 1/8" and 1/16" ribbons; #4, #8, and #16 Braids; Facets; and silk threads Soie Perlee; and Soie Gobelin. Kreinik Mfg. Co. Inc., P.O. Box 1966, Parkersburg, WV 26102

• YLI 100% Cotton Quilting Thread, Select 100% long-staple cotton thread, Basting & Bobbin Thread, Size 30 Silk Thread, Size 50 Silk Thread, and Pearl Crown Rayon. YLI Corporation, 161 West Main St., Rock Hill, SC 29830

• Sulky size 30 rayon thread

• DMC Antique Gold and Silver Embroidery Thread

Among the many other products used:
• Artemis Exquisite Embellishments' Hanah Silk hand-dyed ribbons. Artemis, 179 High St., So. Portland, ME 04106

• Things Japanese Colorhue Instant Set Silk Dyes. Things Japanese, 9805 NE 116th Ste. 7160, Kirkland, WA 98034-4248

Table of Contents

Introduction

Crazy quilting most often consists of placing patches of fancy fabrics onto a foundation layer of muslin and securing them in place with embroidery and embellishments. As with all types of quilting, variations can and do occur.

You may notice this definition does not include a form the crazy quilt should take, but instead elaborates upon the process. Crazy quilts of the past were made up of whole-quilt patched tops, or the quilting was divided into blocks or strips. Some featured a medallion-like center, while some sported fanciful borders. Some had much embroidery, others none. Some were embellished, others not. In short, there was no definitive format.

After writing *The Magic of Crazy Quilting* (Krause Publications, 1998), a book of mainly by-hand methods, I felt compelled to stretch my understanding of this artful quilt style and continue my exploration beyond the ideas presented there; namely, to seek machine interpretations of embellishments and embroidery and further explore the design of the quilt itself. Wanting to pursue machine work was a **big** change for one who had previously stated "I'd rather do it by hand."

Those words, and the idea of creating designs for crazy quilts, are what pushed this book into existence. This became a personal challenge. I was suddenly inspired and filled with new thoughts and ideas, resulting in many sketches and a notebook that was quickly filled with quilt designs and machine embellishment ideas. I then began to try different threads, machine feet and settings, stabilizers, and techniques. All of this fueled new fires—and it became fun. Happily, I discovered that the machine only **assists** in creativity, and that the workhorse behind it all is still the creative mind. I had not given myself up to the machine after all.

Although a crazy quilt can be made entirely by machine, many of the quilts in this book are a combination of machine and hand work. Combining machine with hand techniques tremendously expands ones repertoire of embellishment possibilities. The two combine well, can be used interchangeably, and both, in my opinion, are adventures worth exploring.

I love crazy quilting. The richness of the colors, the stitches, and the luxury fabrics incite constant adoration. The design-without-restraint manner of assembly provides endless intrigue. The challenge of beginning with a basketful of materials and ending with something completely different from what was expected can never be underestimated. And finishing a quilt is always an accomplish-

The Bullions & Battenberg wool crazy quilt displayed in the rose garden.

ment of which one can be proud. Regardless of doing by machine or by hand, this is what it's all about.

As examples of how one's surroundings can influence quilt designs, embroidery, and embellishments, I've included a few floral portraits from my garden and some scenes from my beloved home state, Maine. Many of the quilts in this book were inspired by just these things. Let the photos suggest color schemes, forms for appliqué, ribbonworks, and other embellishments in your work. You may also like to look to your own area for similar inspiration.

How to Use This Book

First, browse through Part 1 and familiarize yourself with the patching/piecing methods and the various designs. For a design you wish to make, read through the instructions before beginning. The instructions for each quilt are given according to the quilt that is shown, but because crazy quilting is, by its very

nature, a creative endeavor, feel totally free to make changes according to your intuition or preference. Creative Notes following each design propose a few of the many possible adaptations.

Next, peruse Part 2, and for this section, sit down at your sewing machine and try the techniques using scrap fabrics; if these turn out well, they can be saved to be used as crazy patches. Be willing to experiment. Purchase a selection of interesting threads and other materials that are called for and allow yourself to freely play.

Information on how to assemble and finish a quilt appears in Part 3.

Machine embroidery can be used on the quilts where I have done handwork. If you wish to embroider by hand as I have, a sampling of hand embroidery stitches are diagrammed and explained in Part 4. *Crazy Quilts by Machine* does not retell the many hand techniques for embroidery and embellishments that are already covered in *The Magic of Crazy Quilting*. I hope you will treasure both books as integral to your needlework ideas collection.

I hope too that you make many wonderful discoveries in your exploration of crazy quilting, whether by hand or machine. My advice is simple: follow your heart and your dreams. Crazy quilting is an artful process; if you let it, it will happen. Enjoy!

J.M.M.

I define patching as fastening a patch of fabric to a background fabric, such as a foundation. Quilters who are trying crazy quilting after years of doing traditional piecing often seem baffled by the patching process. Patching is neither easier nor more difficult, but is different. Being different, it becomes necessary to "bend" one's thinking and planning to a new way of doing. Piecing, to me, means to sew two pieces of fabric together, resulting in a seam between them, and without background fabric.

Some quilters have distinguished between quilts that are "quilted" and those that are "tied," placing crazy quilts into the "tied" category. I would like to differ on this point. Most crazy quilts are both: the patches are quilted by embroidery and embellishments to the foundation layer, while these two layers are held to the backing with ties. The foundation fabric used in most crazy quilts is a substitute for the batting used in traditional quilts.

Of the four crazy quilting methods in this book, only one, Confetti, is "piecing." The remaining three are "patching." The Confetti quilts can be traditionally machine quilted through all layers, while the patched quilts are both quilted and tied.

Getting Started

Here is some basic information to get started. Additional tools and materials are given in Part 2. Refer to each quilt design for other specifics.

Workspace

An efficient workspace consists of a sewing desk or table next to an ironing board that is lowered to the table's or desk's height. You should be able to turn from the sewing machine to use the iron without leaving the chair. For safety, position the iron by an outlet.

Nearby, on a table or the floor, allow space for a cutting mat at least 24" x 36" to be used with a rotary cutter for accurate cutting of binding, backing, and border fabrics and for the Confetti method.

Fabrics

Fabric types are suggested for each quilt design. To make a Confetti quilt, choose mainly quilting cottons, available at any quilting store, in a combination of printed and solid colors. You may also add one or two other cotton types of similar weight, including cotton flannel.

To make crazy quilts of fancy fabrics, first assemble a collection of fabrics. Solids are preferred over prints because embroidery and embellishments usually add plenty of ornament. Collect plain and textured fabrics, including sateen, chintz, velveteen, moirés, jacquards, and damasks. For ease of handling,

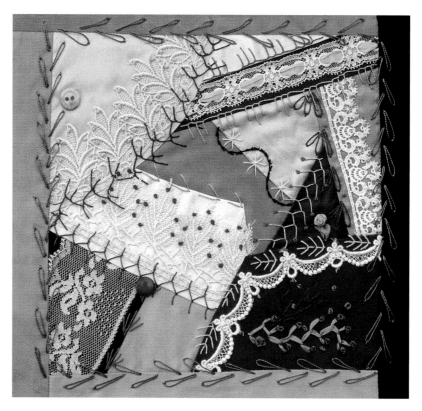

choose fabrics made of natural fibers and of rayon or acetate. Fabrics made of 100-percent cotton include velveteen, chintz, sateen, and damask. Fabrics made of acetate include satin, taffeta, and moiré taffeta. Many of these can be found in regular fabric stores, while others can be found in drapery and upholstery shops.

Trims

Cotton and rayon laces and Venices always seem to have a place on a fancy crazy quilt. Also, collect a variety of trims such as soutache,

cordings, gimpes, braids, and a selection of fabric ribbons in various widths. Laces can be sewn into seams as the quilt is patched, and other ribbons and trims can be sewn across patches or along the edges of seams.

Foundation Fabrics

The most used fabric for crazy quilt foundations is a quality cotton muslin. This provides a firm base which helps keep the work smooth. Cotton batiste can be used to make a lightweight quilt, while silk organza can be used for a silk quilt.

Patched crazy quilts require a foundation upon which to lay the patches. A Confetti pieced quilt does not normally use one.

Tools

In addition to a sewing machine (covered below), the following tools—some of which you may already have—are basic to all types of machine sewing:

- 7" or 8" shears
- Trimmers or embroidery scissors
- Seam ripper
- Straight pins
- Tape measure
- A separate scissors to be used for cutting paper that is not used for cutting fabric (paper dulls scissors).

For Confetti piecing and accurate cutting of binding, backing, and border fabric:

- Rotary cutter
- 24" x 36" cutting mat
- Acrylic gridded ruler for use with a rotary cutter

Sewing Machine

This book is for any basic sewing machine that does forward and reverse straight stitching, zigzag, and darning.

Sit down with your sewing machine, its manual, some scrap fabrics and threads, and try all of the gizmos and settings the machine has and is capable of. This is the single most important thing you can do when getting started. Many of the techniques given in the manual can be used in creating patches for crazy quilts. Keep the manual handy for looking up recommended settings when needed.

Follow the manufacturer's recommendations for matching needle sizes to threads and fabrics and, above all, keep the machine well cleaned (and oiled if necessary), especially the bobbin area. A dull needle can also cause stitching problems, so keep a supply on hand and change them as needed.

Preparation

If you are making a quilt that is to be washable, pre-wash all fabrics. Although most cottons can be machine washed and dried, fancier types such as satin, taffeta, and silks should be gently washed by hand in lukewarm water and mild soap (not detergent)

and line dried.

Always be sure to wash foundation fabrics. Cotton muslin and silk organza may be prone to shrinkage. Dry, press, and trim off any selvages that prevent the fabric from lying flat.

If your fabrics are labeled "dry clean only," this is usually because washing could cause fading of a surface finish, the dyes to run, or shrinkage. By hand, test-wash a small piece to see whether changes occur.

It is a good idea to wash any trims and laces that will be used and to test embroidery threads to see if the dyes run. Wet a length of thread and lay it on a damp paper towel. If dye bleeds out, save the thread for a non-washable project.

Pressing

Often, instructions call for pressing or lightly pressing. Some fancy fabrics may scorch or melt, so first test the iron on a small piece of the fabric. It is often the best policy to simply use a "warm" iron temperature. Use a press cloth if pressing leaves a shine on fabrics. You can make a press cloth by hemming a yard of 44" wide washed cotton muslin. Press; do not slide the iron around. Patched and embroidered pieces may be pressed by laying them face-down on a terry cloth towel. This prevents flattening the work.

Part 1
Four Methods and Quilts to Make

Method 1: Using Patterns

Following the guidelines provided by patterns is an easy way to get started if you haven't yet tried crazy quilting. This is a way to become familiar with the concept and still create a beautiful crazy quilt. Use this method for your first quilt or two, then move on to any of the other methods in this book.

The three quilt projects in this section are presented in order of additions to them; a greater number of embellishments are added to each consecutive quilt. Observe the photos to see how added embellishments change the surface of a quilt. The Earthtones Throw features a dignified simplicity in com-parison to Monet's Garden, which is more decorative with its added laces. Ribbonwork, sewn-on buttons, and yet more complex embellishments on the Rambling Roses quilt add further dimensionality.

Patterns for six blocks, to be enlarged on a photocopier, appear on pages 24-29. If you would like, you may instead create block drawings of your own. Prepare a sheet of paper the size of the block you wish to make. Next, sketch lines to indicate the patches, making them the sizes and shapes of your preference. Finally, pro-ceed with the instructions on the following page, ignoring the enlarging.

Project Difficulty Levels: Easy projects are designed for the beginner and Intermediate projects are somewhere in-between Easy and Challenging, which is a project that has some complexity to it.

Note: Refer to Part 3 for additional information on how to assemble and finish quilts and Part 4 for basic hand-embroidery stitch instructions.

Instructions for Sewing Blocks

Tools needed:
- Photocopier
- Scissors for paper
- Pins
- Shears for cutting fabric
- Sewing machine

1. Enlarge the block pattern of your choice using a photocopier: enlarge 150 percent to make a 9" square or 200 percent to make a 12" square block.

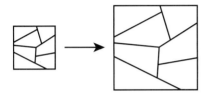

Cut out the paper pattern pieces.
You will need a square of foundation fabric for each block, patch fabrics, and sewing thread.

2. One piece at a time, lay the pattern onto a patch fabric with right sides facing up. Pin. Cut around the pattern piece, adding a seam allowance; an allowance of about 3/8" up to 1/2" is desirable. As you cut the patches, lay them in their correct places following the block diagram in this book.

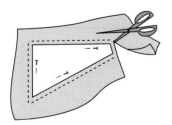

3. By machine, sew the patches onto the foundation fabric in the same order they are numbered.

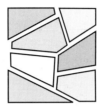

a. Place Piece 1 onto the foundation and pin.
b. With right sides together, lay the second piece onto the first. Sew it to the first through all layers, open out the patch, and press.

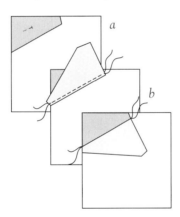

c. Continue to add pieces in the order they are numbered. If desired, sew lace into some of the seams. Occasionally, a final patch will have two edges needing to be sewn. Machine sew one of them. Fold under the remaining edge, press, pin, and baste. Later, use embroidery to hold the edge in place.
4. Several of the block designs given here include an appliquéd patch such as a circle or rectangle. Press its seam allowances under, pin, and hand-baste in place to be secured by embroidery later.

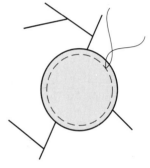

Once the patches are sewn and before the quilt top is assembled, the individual blocks can be treated to all of the embroidery and embellishments you'd like to add.

Easy

Earthtones Throw

Here is a throw of cotton fabrics that will be a pleasure to snuggle up in as autumn leaves begin to fall. Delightfully simple to make, this cozy wrap in soft neutral colors consists of only one of the block patterns (choose one!), with the colors arranged differently from one block to the next. Hand embroidery provides further variation while adding a rich, textural quality to the quilt. An antique gold border accentuates the earthy colors, rimmed by a beige tassel trim. Cotton flannel provides a thin batting.

Although I have used hand embroidery in the quilt shown here, you can substitute Patch Seam Embroidery (see Part 2, page 122) using pearl cotton. You may also choose to add some of the embellishments given in Part 2, although if this is your first project, you may well opt for simplicity and add only embroidery. In case you choose to add embellishments, do so before the blocks are sewn together. Individual blocks are far easier to work on than a whole quilt top.

Size: 64" square (36 9" square blocks and 5" borders). (This throw can also be made 55" square with 25 blocks, or 46" square with 16 blocks. Adapt the yardage amounts given on the following page to reflect the difference in size.)

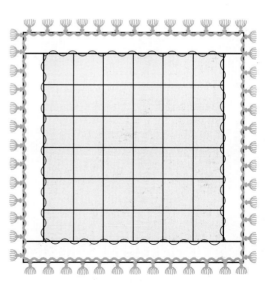

The Earthtones Throw nestled between blue-leaved Hosta and Columbine by a rock wall.

Palette

Patch colors include: medium shades of taupe, rose-brown, rose-peach, antique gold, and pastel shades of cream, silver, beige, and peach.

Embroidery threads used include medium to light shades of yellow, green, orange, and orchid.

Materials

(All fabrics 44" wide)
- 3/4 yard each of seven 100-percent cotton fabrics such as: sateen, chintz, broadcloth, lightweight twill, in the above colors
- 3-1/2 yards of muslin
- 2 yards of cotton sateen in antique gold
- 4 yards of cotton flannel fabric
- 4 yards of cotton backing fabric
- 7-1/2 yards of 1-1/2" wide cotton/acetate tassel fringe
- Size 8 pearl cotton in the colors listed above
- Size 8 pearl cotton in light orange

Note: Use 1/4" seam allowances for assembly.

Cutting

1. Cut 36 muslin foundations, each 9-1/2" square.

2. Out of antique gold cotton sateen, cut two side borders, each 5-1/2" x 54-1/2", and top and bottom borders, each 5-1/2" x 64-1/2". Cut the remaining muslin the same, place on the backs of the borders, and handle the two as one.

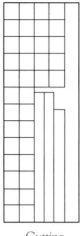

Cutting diagram for muslin.

3. Cut and sew the flannel to make one piece, 64-1/2" square. Do the same for the backing fabric.

Making the Quilt Top

1. Enlarge Block 3 (see page 26), or the block of your choice, 150 percent on a photocopier and cut out the pieces.

Method for Cutting the Patches

1. Stack all seven fabrics evenly. Using a sharp shears or a rotary cutter, lay on the pattern pieces and cut out each piece through all layers, adding 1/4" (or more) seam

allowances to each. Keeping the stacks intact, place the pieces in their numbered order.

In order to have each block different, proceed as follows. Onto one of the 9-1/2" muslin squares, place the top color from Stack 1. (Refer to Instructions for Sewing Blocks, page 11, for sewing instructions.)

Take the second color from Stack 2, placing the top color to the bottom of the stack. Sew it onto the block. Then, take the third color from Stack 3, placing the two above it to the bottom of the stack, and sew it on. Continue in this way to complete the first block. To sew the next block, simply use the topmost color from each stack. Continue until all seven blocks are sewn.

Repeat as above to sew 35 blocks. Cut pieces individually to make an additional block.

2. The patch seams of each block may be machine or hand embroidered. Refer to Patch Seam Embroidery on page 122 for machine embroidery or to Part 4 for hand embroidery stitch instructions.

3. Sew the blocks together following instructions in Part 3. Work Blanket Stitch along the block seams with light orange pearl cotton.

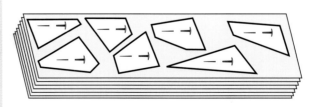

Finishing the Quilt

(Refer to Part 3 for quilt finishing instructions.)

1. Sew on the borders. Work machine Patch Seam Embroidery or meandering Outline Stitch by hand along the inner edge of the border with light orange pearl cotton.

2. Using the flannel in place of batting, add the backing and assemble the quilt with a Knife-edge finish (see page 134). Tie the quilt by hand using pearl cotton in the color of your choice (see page 135).

3. Machine-sew the tassel trim onto the outer edges of the border, making a fold in the header of the trim at each corner in order to turn the corners neatly.

Stones at the beach are colorful neutral tones.

Creative Notes

• Choose colors found in the sky, ocean, pebbles, forest, or meadow to make a similar quilt in a different color scheme.

• If you are adept at machine quilting, this quilt can be made without embroidery and free-motion quilted using the thread of your choice.

• Make the throw bed-size for a year 'round bed covering. See page 142 for standard sizes for bed quilts.

Monet's Garden, a Floor Pillow

Rich greens and vivid iris shades combine in an Impressionistic garden-like effect, enlivened by machine and hand embroidery and set off by dramatic Venice laces and motifs. The fabric colors may seem bold and unusual, but they are an expected combination in the perennial garden and go together with ease. Look closely at the machine embroidered details to see nearly translucent-winged bugs tangled in the foliage, some orange, others yellow. Bright touches of embroidery suggest butterflies, flower centers, spiderwebs, and other bits of nature.

The whole of this interplay appears to mimic the jumble of leaf and flower patterns in the garden. From a distance, everything blends, and one gains a whole different perspective that is based on the color scheme itself, much like viewing floral gardens from afar. As in many examples of crazy quilting, the viewer will have one impression when seeing the quilt from afar, and quite another when close-up. The more details added, the greater this effect will be.

This project goes a step beyond the Earthtones Throw, by adding laces into seams, creating a richer effect. Machine embroidery, because it is flat, tends to recede into the background, allowing the dimensionality of Venice laces and touches of hand work to grandly step forward. The pillow is finished with a luxurious cotton brush fringe.

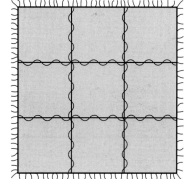

Size: 27" square (nine 9" square blocks), not including the fringe. For a smaller, 18" square pillow, make four blocks, adjusting the yardages on the following page.

The colors of Monet's Garden pillow blend with the surrounding iris and poppies.

Palette

The colors in this pillow are based on one of the fabrics used, a print in shades of green, purple, black, and silver. Beige was added to the mix as a neutral tone. Except for the one print, all of the fabrics are plain.

Embroidery threads used include yellow, gold, rust, orange, blue, green, gray, purple, and deep red.

Materials

(All fabrics 44" wide)
- Scraps or small amounts of fabrics, including 100-percent cottons: velveteen, chintz, sateen; and acetate satin in the above colors
- 3 yards of muslin
- Cotton and rayon Venice edgings and motifs and cotton eyelet lace
- Size 50 100-percent cotton sewing threads in greens, yellow, and orange
- Size 8 pearl cotton in the colors listed above
- 1 yard of drapery or decorator cotton backing fabric
- 3-1/8 yards of 1-1/2" heavy cotton brush fringe in dark green
- Stuffing
- Optional: Velcro or sew-on snaps

Note: Use 1/2" seam allowances for assembly.

Cutting

1. Cut the muslin into nine 10" squares for the block foundations and two 28" squares to make the pillow insert that will contain the stuffing. Cut the backing fabric into two pieces, each 18" x 28".

Making the Pillow Top

1. Use all six block patterns (three of them will be used twice) and enlarge them 150 percent on a photocopier.

2. Prepare and sew nine blocks, following the instructions on page 11. Add cotton eyelet laces into some of the seams.

3. Working freehand, machine-embroider zigzag leaves, the

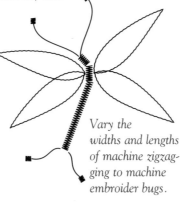

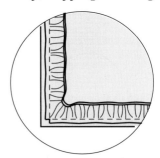

Vary the widths and lengths of machine zigzagging to machine embroider bugs.

Dot Stitch (see page 124), and bugs, as shown in the diagram here, using cotton sewing thread. Hand-embroider along patch seams, adding French Knots (see page 140) to some of the rows. Vary the thread colors and add embroidery until the blocks appear finished.

4. Sew the blocks together and press the seams open. By hand, embroider meandering Outline Stitch along each seam, keeping the seam allowances open and flat, or use machine Patch Seam Embroidery (see page 122), meandering the stitching along seams.

Finishing the Pillow

1. With right sides together, pin the brush fringe to the pillow top, clipping the fringe

header to neatly turn at each corner. Butt the ends together, but do not overlap them. Machine-baste the fringe to the pillow top.

2. Hem one 28" end of each backing piece by turning under 1/4" twice and machine stitching. Overlap the hemmed ends, and place the backing right sides together with the pillow top. Sew completely around. Turn the pillow right side out.

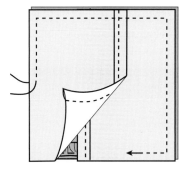

3. To make the pillow insert, place the 28" muslin squares together and sew around, leaving an opening for stuffing. Turn right side out. Stuff tightly for a firm pillow, or loosely for a floppy one. Sew the opening shut. Insert into pillow cover. Velcro or sew-on snaps may be added to the overlapped pillow cover.

Pair brilliant blues or fuchsia with greens and neutrals for a colorful scheme.

Creative Notes

• To make a similar pillow in a different color scheme, choose several shades of your favorite flower color and add greens and neutrals; this makes a complete color scheme whether you choose yellows, oranges, purples, reds, or blues. Combine vivids and pastels, or try all pastels.
• Assembling a color scheme is easy by first choosing a print fabric, then adding a selection of matching solids.

Easy

Rambling Roses

This classically Victorian-style crazy quilt features deep-green velveteen sashings with bouffant ribbonwork roses at its intersections. The lush green suggests hedgerows in a floriferous countryside setting, jewel tones used for many of the patches tend to mellow under the green's influence, and the whole seems evocative of an era gone by.

A design such as this is brought together by the richness of its embroidery and embellishments. These additions not only provide a softening touch to the angularity of patch seams, but also integrate the quilt top as a whole. This is not to suggest that the quilt surface should be crowded, but that sufficient detail be added until each block appears complete on its own. If you question how much to add, just keep adding until the block feels like a finished piece. At that point, you will find yourself questioning, "Do I really need any more?"

Despite its fancy appearance, this quilt is easy to make. All six of the block patterns are used, with three of them used twice. Building on the techniques used in the previous two projects, additional embellishments are added, including insets and ribbonwork, to create a more dimensional surface.

Size: 51-1/2" square (nine 12" blocks, 2" sashings, and 5-3/4" wide borders).

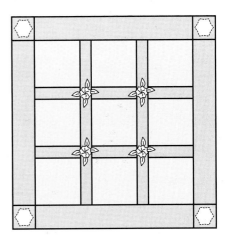

The Rambling Roses quilt shown with antique Alba roses in full bloom.

Palette

Fabrics include dark shades: burgundy, red, black, navy, browns, and yellow-gold. The light shades are: blue, rose, cream, gray, yellow, and beige. Several of the fabrics are soft prints.

Embroidery thread colors used include burgundy, bright pink, violet, gray, gold, peach, and green.

Materials

(All fabrics 44" wide)

• Scraps or small amounts of fabrics, including 100-percent cottons: velveteen, sateen, chintz; acetates such as: moiré, satin, taffeta; and moiré bengaline in the above colors
• 1-1/4 yards of cotton velveteen in dark green
• 1-1/8 yards of muslin
• Venice and other laces, wired ribbons, photo transfers, and silk ribbons for embroidery
• Size 8 pearl cotton in the colors listed above
• Size 8 pearl cotton in medium jade
• 3 yards of 44" wide backing fabric, or 1-1/2 yards of 60" wide
• 4 lace motifs, 4" in diameter
• 6 yards of self-made or purchased binding

Photo transfers: I used a photo transfer paper, taking it to a color photocopier and copying cut-outs from antique postcards onto it. Then I ironed them onto silk satin fabric according to the manufacturer's instructions.

Note: Use 1/4" seam allowances for assembly.

Cutting

1. Cut nine 12-1/2" squares of muslin for foundations. Out of the dark green velveteen, cut four borders, each 6" x 40-1/2", four 6" square corner blocks, six 2-1/2" x 12-1/2" spacers, and two 2-1/2" x 40-1/2" sashings.

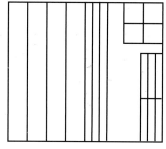

Cutting diagram for velveteen

Note: When sewing on the velveteen borders, spacers, and sashings, have the nap of the velveteen running the same direction throughout. The nap should run upwards (it feels smoother when you stroke the pile moving upwards) on vertical pieces, and either to the left or the right on all horizontal pieces.

Making the Quilt Top

1. Use all six block patterns (three are used twice) and enlarge them 200 percent on a photocopier. Adding laces into some of the seams, patch the foundations according to the instructions on page 11.

2. By machine, appliqué the photo transfers and sew Insets (see page 125) into some of the patches. Use machine Patch Seam Embroidery (see page 122) to stitch a row of pearl cotton along each patch seam.

3. Add hand embroidery along the rows of pearl cotton. Machine-stitch a spiderweb (see page 123), do some silk ribbon embroideries by machine (see page 132), ribbonworked flowers (see page 131), and Broderie Perse (see page 128). I have included other details by hand, including ribbonwork, sewn-on buttons, beads, and lace motifs.

Finishing the Quilt

1. Sew the blocks, spacers, and sashings together according to the directions in Part 3, and following the diagram of the quilt on page 21. Hand-embroider Straight Stitch into fan-like shapes along the seams of the spacers and the sashings using jade pearl cotton. Refer to Part 4 for hand embroidery stitches or use machine Patch Seam Embroidery along the seams.

2. Sew two borders to opposite sides of the quilt. Add a corner block to each end of the remaining borders, sew one to the top, and one to the bottom of the quilt. Baste a 4" diameter lace motif onto each corner block and work French Knots to fasten them in place. Work Straight Stitch fans along the border seams.

3. Add the backing, tie, and bind the quilt according to the directions in Part 3. (The quilt shown was bound with cotton velveteen cut on the straight grain.)

Creative Notes

Seven Sisters, a favorite antique rose, rambles freely over the arbor.

• This is an excellent project for exploring embellishment methods and color combinations. Really experiment with these things, putting yourself right into it and letting the piece grow as it will—and have fun! It is as important to enjoy the process as it is to appreciate the outcome.

• A richly embellished crazy quilt is a natural candidate for a wall hanging. Sew a rod pocket to the top of the backing and insert a dowel for hanging (see page 136). Made larger, this design would make a lovely bed coverlet by eliminating hard trims (such as buttons) and making the required number of blocks for the size of the bed.

The Block Patterns

See the instructions for using the block patterns on page 11.

Block 1

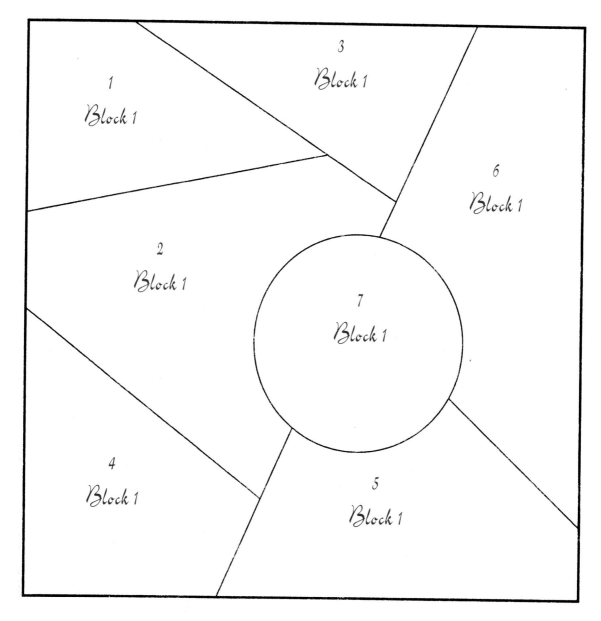

1
Block 1

3
Block 1

6
Block 1

2
Block 1

7
Block 1

4
Block 1

5
Block 1

Block 2

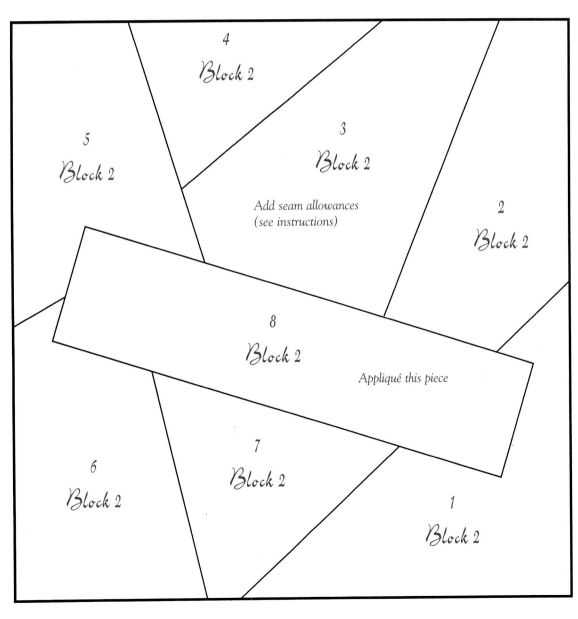

4
Block 2

3
Block 2

5
Block 2

Add seam allowances
(see instructions)

2
Block 2

8
Block 2

Appliqué this piece

6
Block 2

7
Block 2

1
Block 2

Block 3

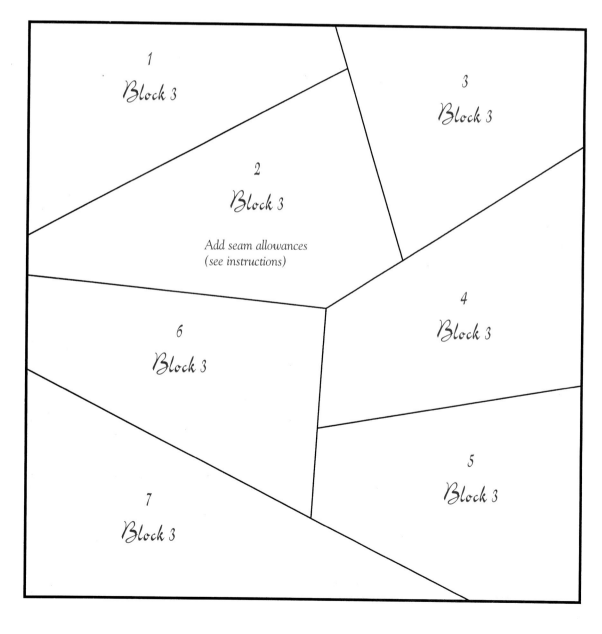

1

Block 3

3

Block 3

2

Block 3

Add seam allowances
(see instructions)

4

Block 3

6

Block 3

5

Block 3

7

Block 3

Block 4

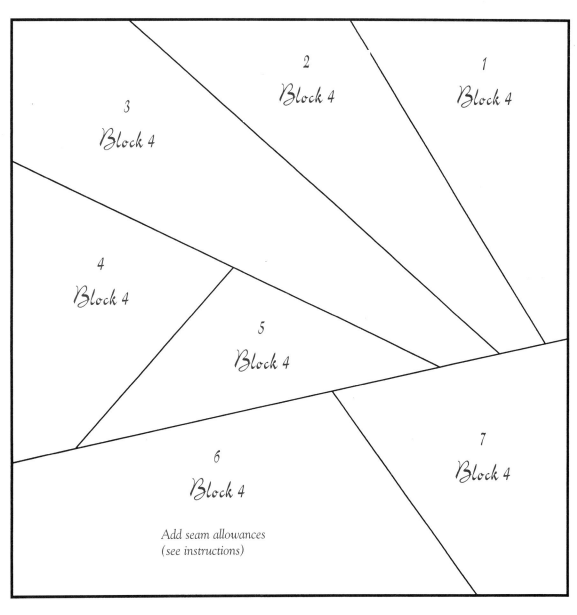

3
Block 4

2
Block 4

1
Block 4

4
Block 4

5
Block 4

7
Block 4

6
Block 4

Add seam allowances
(see instructions)

Block 5

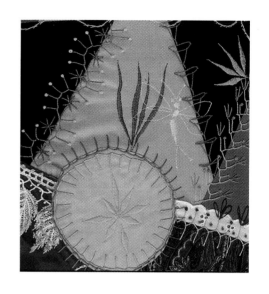

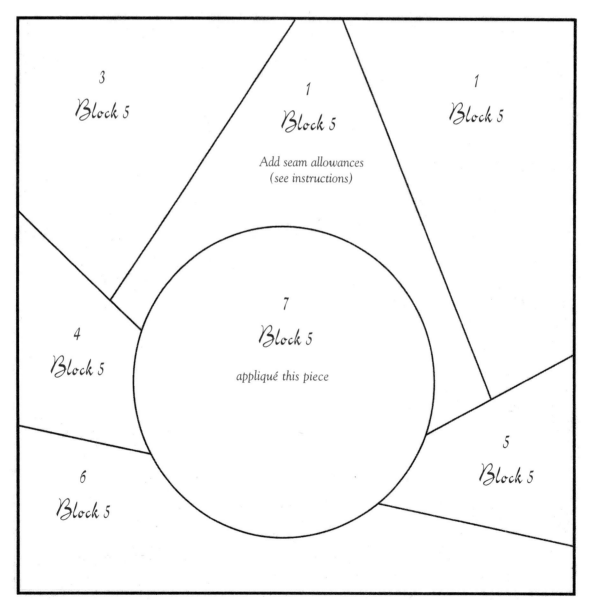

3
Block 5

1
Block 5

Add seam allowances
(see instructions)

1
Block 5

7
Block 5

appliqué this piece

4
Block 5

5
Block 5

6
Block 5

Block 6

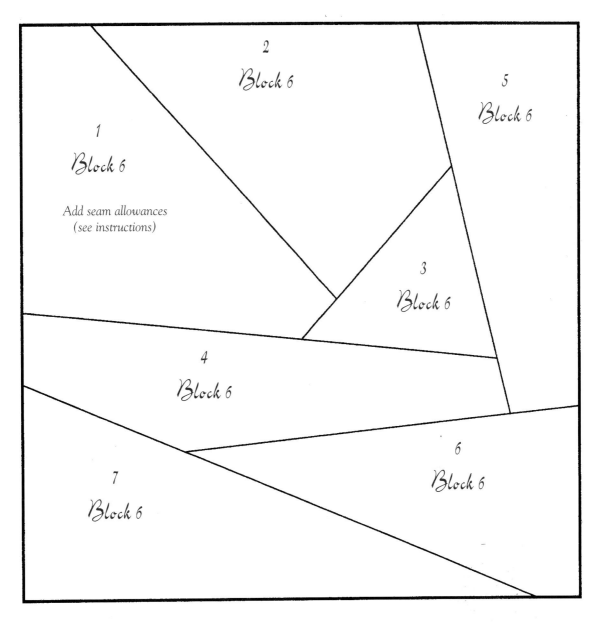

2
Block 6

5
Block 6

1
Block 6

Add seam allowances
(see instructions)

3
Block 6

4
Block 6

6
Block 6

7
Block 6

Method 2: Topstitch Appliqué

Topstitch Appliqué is a natural for those who have been using the "Antique" method of laying crazy quilt patches by hand that is explained in my first book, The Magic of Crazy Quilting. *The same as the by-hand method, it involves placing the patches onto a foundation and folding the overlapping edges under. The difference is that trims are laid along the patch edges and are machine-sewn in place instead of being basted and embroidered. In one line of stitching, a patch is both secured and decorated.*

This method retains the beautiful effects of hand patching, including the folded edges of patches and the ease with which curved edges can be used. When laces are used as trims, the result is a frothy "wedding cake" look. Adding additional embroidery and embellishments is purely optional.

The three "wedding cake" quilts in this section incorporate fancy fabrics in interpretations of traditional patchwork designs. These quilts suggest how crazy quilting can be incorporated into geometric styles of patchwork, while demonstrating how embellishments can be used to enhance an otherwise plain surface.

In the second part of this section are variations of the Topstitch Appliqué Method, demonstrating how it can be applied to making a blue jeans quilt and a wool quilt.

Trims for Topstitch Appliqué

Suitable trims include cotton and rayon Venice laces, cotton cluny laces, woven braids, upholstery gimpes, ricrac, ribbons, and lace insertions. Quality cotton and rayon Venices and laces can be found where bridal and heirloom sewing supplies are sold. Crocheted, knitted, tatted, bobbin, and other fine handmade laces may also be used.

Instructions for Topstitch Appliqué

Tools needed:
- Pins
- Shears for cutting fabric
- Iron and ironing board
- Sewing machine

1. Begin with foundation fabric the size of the piece needed plus seam allowances. Cut out a patch the size and shape of your choice, noting shapes and sizes of patches in the diagrams and photos in this section. Refer to the quilt patterns for suggested fabric colors. Beginning anywhere on the foundation, lay the patch and pin. Cut out and add the next patch, having it overlap an inch onto the first, and pin. Continue to cut and lay patches, having them overlap at least an inch, until the foundation is covered.

2. Place the block on the ironing board. Begin anywhere on the block, such as at one corner, and, working progressively over the entire block, one patch at a time, fold, and press under the overlapped edge 1/2". Then, check that the foundation is adequately covered. You may need to adjust patches and even add a patch or two if any gaps have occurred.

3. Lay trims along the folded and pressed edges of the patches and pin. Position the trims so the machine stitching will be about 1/4" from the patch's folded edge. Lay trims on the entire block before sewing. An occasional patch edge can be left untrimmed but basted, to be fastened with embroidery later.

4. Sew along each trim using matching thread. Do not backstitch. Look for and sew the most underlapped patch available each time. Bring the thread ends to the back and tie off (see page 121).

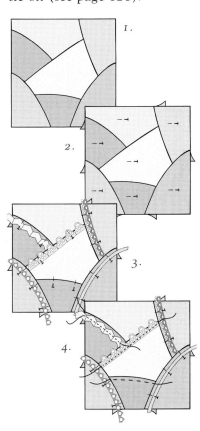

5. Press the block, having it face down on a terry cloth towel. Baste around the outer edges. Add embroidery and embellishments as desired, completing them before the blocks are sewn together to make the quilt top.

Note: If pinning and sewing are done carefully and some light pressing is done on the piece in progress, there should be no "shrinkage" of the foundation. If your work tends to shrink, cut the foundation pieces slightly larger than needed, trimming the sewn piece to size afterwards.

Three "Wedding Cake" Quilts

The following three "wedding cake" quilts are given a fancy appearance through the combination of fancy fabrics and the trims used. I have chosen to add small amounts of hand embroidery and silk ribbon embroidery as additional enhancements. You may substitute machine embellishments from Part 2 if you prefer.

Easy

Elegant Octagons Table Runner

Whether for tea or fine dining, this runner dresses the table in grand style. The octagon blocks create a shaped edge, here trimmed with a lustrous rayon cording. Hand embroidery, lacy motifs, and touches of silk ribbon embroidery further enhance this piece.

Size: 15" wide x 70" long. I used 20 octagons. (Measure the length of your table and use the appropriate number of octagons to fit, including a one-half to one-block drop at each end. Adapt the yardages on the following page if necessary.)

The Elegant Octagons Table Runner takes center stage at teatime.

Palette

Light and pastel colors, including green, rose, peach, lilac, cream, and gray, are used with white and off-white. Together, they give this piece its heirloom character.

Thread colors include pastel shades of the same colors.

Materials

(All fabrics 44" wide)
- Scraps or small pieces of assorted fabrics, including cotton/rayon bengaline; 100-percent cottons: velveteen and chintz; acetates such as satin and taffeta; and and silk noil in the colors listed above
- 1 yard of muslin
- 1/8 yard of bengaline for insets
- Cotton and rayon trims and laces in white and off-white to be used for Topstitch Appliqué
- Size 8 pearl cotton in the colors listed above
- Size 8 pearl cotton in light gold
- 1 yard of backing fabric
- 7 yards of rayon cording
- Size 50 100-percent cotton sewing threads to match trims and laces
- Venice motifs, silk ribbon for embroidery, and other embellishments as desired to be added after the blocks are patched

Note: Use 1/4" seam allowances for assembly.

Cutting

1. Trace and cut out the paper patterns for the octagon and inset. Cut 20 octagons out of muslin (or the number required for your table). Fold the muslin and place the octagon pattern on the fold in order to make complete octagons.

2. Cut nine insets out of bengaline, or the number needed for your runner size. Cut the same number out of muslin and place one muslin piece on the back of each inset; handle the two as one.

Cheerful English Daisies suggest shapes that may fit together, such as octagons.

Making the Table Runner

1. Topstitch Appliqué the muslin octagon foundations, adding the cotton and rayon trims and laces according to the instructions on page 31. Baste around the edges of each block. Add embroidery and embellishments as desired. Refer to the runner photo for suggested embellishments.

2. Machine-sew the octagon blocks together without sewing into the seam allowances at the seam ends. For ease and accuracy, it is recommended that insets be added by hand as follows instead of sewing them in by machine: Turn under the block edges where the inset will be added and press. Place the inset under the opening. Pin and baste, then slipstitch invisibly by hand all around.

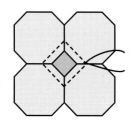

Airy columbines bob at the ends of long stems in the early summer garden.

3. Hand-embroider Feather Stitch along the seams. With right sides together and using the runner as a pattern, cut out the backing fabric the same shape as the runner. Sew around, leaving an opening for turning. Trim seams, turn right side out, and lightly press. Hand-stitch cording all around, then slipstitch the opening, concealing the ends of the cording inside of the seam.

Creative Notes

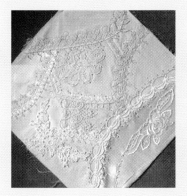

A 12" octagon in heirloom whites and off-whites.

• Enlarge the patterns 150 percent on a photocopier to have 12" octagons and make as many as needed for a bed-size quilt. Worked in whites and ecrus, this would make an elegant heirloom quilt.

Elegant Octagons
Octagon Pattern

Seam allowances included

Elegant Octagons
Inset Pattern

Seam allowances included

Place on fabric fold

Intermediate

Ode to Degas

In some mysterious way, this quilt reminds me of the art of Degas* with its pinky colors and with blocks set on point, seeming like an abstract version of his frilly ballerinas. ("On point" is a quilter's way of saying that the blocks are set diagonally in the quilt.)

Topstitch Appliquéd blocks are attractive insets in this quilt that is styled in the manner of traditional patchwork. Sashings of slipper satin and the high sheen of the rayon embroidery thread impart an elegant, luxurious look. I have used hand embroidery, but you may substitute machine embroidery and embellishments if you prefer. As a finishing touch, the quilt is tied by sewing on buttons and adding small bits of silk ribbon embroidery.

The quilt's border is a daring departure from the norm. Instead of continuing the sage green, pink is used as a soft background for gathered ribbon florals. This unique touch individualizes the quilt. I urge you to go with your instincts; if you feel you'd like to try something out of the norm, by all means go for it!

Size: 82" square (36 10" square blocks and 6" wide borders).

*Edgar Degas, 1834–1917, a French artist who exhibited with the Impressionists, experimented with new forms of painting by trying to capture the effects of light. Impressionism is an art style concurrent with Victorian Crazy Quilting.

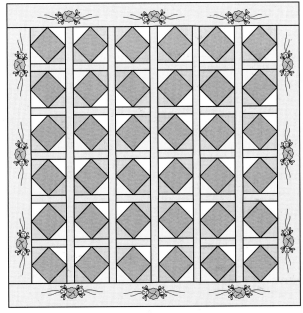

Ode to Degas is a quilt for a romantic setting.

Palette

All shades from pastel to dark are incorporated into this quilt. Choose shades of pinks and purples (three or four of each), adding the neutrals—cream, taupe, and fawn brown—and sage green for sashings. Darks include burgundy, forest green, and black.

Thread colors include gold, pink, teal, fuchsia, violet, blue, yellow, and taupe.

Materials

(All fabrics 44" wide)

- Scraps or small pieces of assorted fabrics, including 100-percent cottons: chintz and velveteen; and acetates such as: moiré, satin, and taffeta in the colors listed above and including 1/4 yard each of four different purples and 1/4 yard each of four different pinks.
- 8-1/2 yards of muslin
- 2-3/4 yards of sage green bridal satin
- 2-3/4 yards of satin border fabric in pink (or sage green to match the sashings)
- 3 spools of Pearl Crown Rayon thread in drab green
- 2 spools of Pearl Crown Rayon thread in lilac
- Pearl Crown Rayon in the colors listed above
- 4-3/4 yards of backing fabric
- 9-1/2 yards of 1/2" wide bias binding, self-made or purchased
- Embellishments such as buttons, silk ribbons for embroidery, and heart-shaped beads
- 5/8" and 1" wide wired rayon ribbons for border florals
- Buttons to sew to the sashings (optional)
- Tracing paper, pencil, scissors

Note: Use 1/4" seam allowances for assembly.

Cutting

1. Out of muslin, cut 36 squares, each 7-1/2", for the central blocks and 36 squares, each 10-1/2", for the large blocks. For Steps 3 and 4, also cut one of muslin for each piece, place the two wrong sides together, and handle as one.

2. Trace and cut out the triangle pattern. Cut 144 triangles out of the 1/4 yards of pinks and purples.

3. Cut the sage green bridal satin into five sashings, each 2-1/2" wide x 70" long. Cut the remaining fabric into 2-1/2" wide strips along the length of the fabric. Cut the strips into 30 spacers, each 10-1/2" long.

4. Out of pink (or sage green) satin, cut four borders, two for the sides, each 6-1/4" x 70-1/2", and two for the top and bottom, each 6-1/4" x 82-1/2".

Making the Quilt Top

Central Blocks

1. Topstitch appliqué the 7-1/2" squares of muslin, adding the cotton and Venice trims and laces according to the instructions on page 31. Baste around the outer edges of each block.

2. Hand-embroider along the patch seams using Pearl Crown Rayon threads in assorted colors and the embroidery stitches of your choice. Add buttons and other embellishments as desired. Refer to the photos for suggested embroidery stitches and embellishments.

Large Block

1. One at a time, fold a 10-1/2" muslin square in half, then fold again in the other direction, and lightly finger-press to make light creases along the folds. Use the creases to accurately center a patched block diagonally on each. Pin.

2. With right sides together, sew two triangles to opposite sides of the central block. Press the seams. Sew on the remaining two triangles in the same manner and press.

3. Carefully trim the muslin away from the back of each central block, leaving a 1/4" seam allowance. Take care to not cut into the patched blocks.

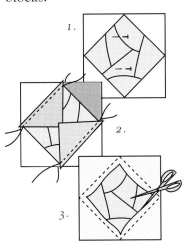

4. With lilac thread, hand-embroider around each central block in meandering Outline Stitch.

Finishing the Quilt

1. Sew the blocks into columns, placing the spacers between the blocks, referring to the diagram on page 37.

2. Sew the columns and sashings together, referring to the diagram on page 37 (and see page 133).

3. Hand-embroider Single Feather Stitch in drab green over the seams of the spacers and sashings. Be sure to work the stitch in the same direction for the entire quilt top. Work the seam under the block toward the right and the seam above the next block (working downward) toward the left. On the sashings, work Single Feather Stitch going downward along one seam, upward along the other.

4. Sew on the borders. Make Gathered Ribbon Flowers (see page 131) by machine, or work ribbon florals by hand, making three of them on each border, and spacing them equally apart. These may be worked freehand, or you may trace the pattern given on page 41 to use as a guide.

5. Add the backing (see page 134). Tie the quilt by sewing on buttons and working silk ribbon embroidery motifs through all layers. Bind the quilt using purchased or self-made binding (see page 134).

Creative Notes

Pale pink old-fashioned roses are beloved cottage garden favorites.

• This design would make a lovely crib quilt made in cotton fabrics and pastel shades. Make it two blocks wide by three blocks long for a small quilt, or three by four for a larger quilt. Use cotton cluny laces and do patch seam embroidery by machine. Instead of ties, quilt by stitching in the ditch.

Ode to Degas
Triangle Pattern

1/4" seam allowances included

Ode to Degas
Border Embroidery Pattern

Center of pattern; work opposite half to match

Abe's Amalgam

Contemporaries of each other, Log Cabin quilts (block-style quilts formed of narrow strips of fabric sewn around a central square and often made of silks) and Crazy Quilts of fancy fabrics were both Victorian-era foundation quilts. The adaptation shown here juxtaposes the two styles by shaping the Log Cabin strips randomly and enlarging the traditionally small center square for crazy patching. One can only imagine Abe Lincoln, log cabin dweller and "Victorian" president, grinning at this amalgam!

Size: 74" square (16 blocks made up of 8" inner blocks set into 15-1/2" blocks and 6" borders).

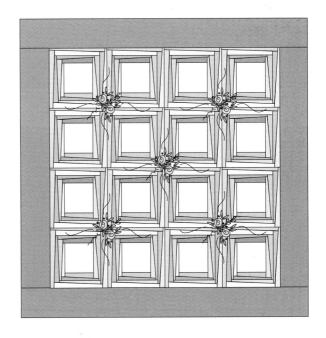

Abe's Amalgam poses on a park bench with a basketful of fresh-cut flowers.

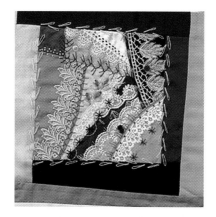

Palette

This quilt consists of a very Victorian mix, including light and dark teal, pink, burgundy, gray, black, white and cream, light and dark purple, and navy. A black border dramatically highlights the rich colors.

Thread colors include burgundy, black, brown, fuchsia, yellow, green, violet, jade, and pink.

Materials

(All fabrics 44" wide)
- 1/2 yard lengths of assorted fabrics, including 100-percent cottons: chintz and broadcloth; and acetates such as satin and taffeta in the colors listed above. Cut two 11" x 18" pieces from each and reserve for Log Cabin patching.
- 6-1/4 yards of muslin
- Cotton and Venice trims and laces in white and off-white to be used for Topstitch Appliqué
- 2-1/4 yards of lightweight satin border fabric in black
- 2-1/4 yards of backing fabric
- 8-1/2 yards of 1/2" wide purchased bias binding or self-made binding
- 7 yards of ecru cotton Venice trim, 1-1/2" wide
- Size 8 pearl cotton in the colors listed above
- Silk ribbons for embroidery and buttons

Note: Use 1/4" seam allowances for assembly.

Cutting

1. From muslin, cut 16 foundation blocks, each 8-1/2" square. Cut 16 additional foundation blocks, each 16" square.

2. Cut two side borders, each 6-1/2" x 62-1/2". Cut a top and a bottom border, each 6-1/2" x 74-1/2". Also cut one of muslin for each piece, place the two wrong sides together, and handle as one.

Making the Quilt Top

Central Blocks

1. Topstitch appliqué the 8-1/2" squares of muslin, adding the cotton and Venice trims and laces according to the instructions on page 31. Baste around the outer edges of each block.

2. Hand-embroider along the patch seams using pearl cot-ton threads in assorted colors and the embroidery stitches of your choice. Add buttons and other embellishments as desired. Refer to the photos for suggested embroidery stitches and embellishments.

Large Block

1. One at a time, fold the 16" muslin square diagonally in half, then fold again in the other direction, and lightly finger-press to make light creases along the folds. Use the creases to accurately center a central block on each. Pin.

2. Work Log Cabin as follows:

a. Take one of the 11" x 18" pieces of fabric and, with right sides together, line it up with one edge of the central block. Sew the seam. So that all strips are long enough, sew along the 18" length of the fabrics. Cut away the excess to leave a random-shaped strip. (To cut the edge straight, first fold the strip, press, and then cut along the fold.) Trim the ends of the strip even with the central block.

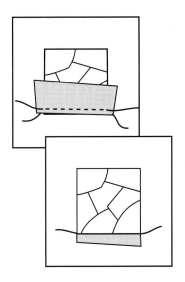

b. Give the block a one-quarter turn. Add the next strip the same way, but sew it onto both the first strip **and** the central block. Open out each strip as it is sewn and press. Continue adding strips, work-

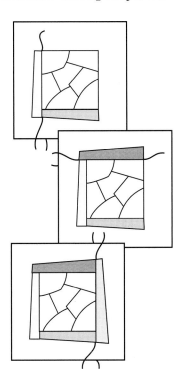

ing clockwise or counter-clockwise (do not reverse direction) and giving the block a one-quarter turn before each.

3. Taking care to not cut through the patched block, trim the extra layer of muslin away from the back of the central block, leaving a 1/4" seam allowance.

4. Hand-embroider around each block using Lazy Daisy or the stitch of your choice (see page 140).

Finishing the Quilt

1. Sew the blocks into columns, referring to the diagram on page 43. Sew the columns together.

2. By hand or machine, work five silk ribbon embroidery motifs at the joins of the blocks, noting the placements on the diagram. These may be worked freehand or you may trace the pattern given on page 47 to use as a guide.

3. Sew on the borders (see page 133).

4. Sew the Venice trim along the border seam by machine, stitching in the ditch. To turn the corners, either gather the trim, or cut the motifs apart. To secure the trim and keep it lying flat, sew down the width of the trim every 4" to 6" or so.

5. Add the backing (see page 134) and tie the quilt, sewing on buttons and working small silk ribbon embroidery motifs through all layers. Bind the quilt using purchased or self-made binding (see page 134).

Creative Notes

A floriferous cottage garden is an inspiring sight.

• This quilt design would be equally effective worked either in all cottons or all silk fabrics. Add more or less embellishments as desired. This design would also make an interesting (and all the more challenging) miniature quilt, by reducing the larger blocks to about 6", with the inner blocks about 3" square.

To embroider roses,
work Outline Stitch in a
circular pattern.

Abe's Amaglam
Embroidery Pattern

for silk ribbon embroidery. Using silk ribbon, see
stitch instructions in Part 4.

Center of pattern;
continue outline
stitching to match
righthand side of
design.

Topstitch Appliqué Variations

The following quilts are variations on the Topstitch Appliqué method. They are adaptations designed specifically for the fabrics that are used. The first is for recycled blue jeans, and the second for a wool quilt.

Easy

Super-easy Blue Jeans Throw

No flipping, fitting, or foundation! This adaptation of the Topstitch Appliqué method requires only sewing and trimming off the excess. What a perfect project for a young person learning how to sew! The finished piece makes an excellent casual throw as is, requiring neither backing nor batting. The method of sewing the throw leaves the fluffy fringes of raveled denim along seams on both right and wrong sides. The eyelet flounce is optional; a bias binding may be used instead.

Size: 56" x 63", not including the eyelet flounce. The six blocks are 28" by 21". Add two blocks to the length to make a twin-size bed blanket or quilt.

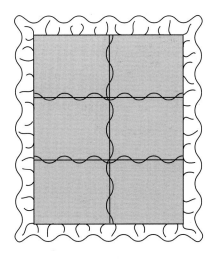

The Super Easy Blue Jeans Throw is a cozy wrap for any sedentary activity.

Palette

Collect worn jeans of any color and trims that will show up against denim. Use thread colors that will show up, such as bright red, yellow, and orange.

Trims to Collect

Choose a variety of washable sew-on trims of your choice. Those used here include ricrac, laces, gimpes, ribbons, green velveteen for appliqué leaves, and floral braids.

Materials

- Well-worn adult-size jeans (eight to nine pairs; you'll need more if using kids' sizes)
- Desired sew-on trims and embellishments (as listed above)
- Floral fabric for Broderie Perse or your choice of bold-printed fabric
- Size 50 100-percent cotton sewing thread in the colors listed above
- Rayon and metallic machine embroidery threads (optional)
- 10 yards of 4" to 5" wide cotton eyelet lace in white (purchase one-and-a-half times the circumference of the quilt)

Making the Throw

1. Prepare the jeans by cutting the good parts away from the seams, pockets, and worn-out parts. Work Broderie Perse (see page 128) on some of these sections, doing approximately 36 appliqués in all. Distribute the appliqués amongst the blocks.

2. Begin with a roughly rectangular piece of denim. Keep the pieces large, about 8" x 10"-12" or so. Cut a second piece to have a rounded or curved edge. Lay the second on the first, overlapping by at least 1". Always keep right sides facing up.

3. Sew the pieces together, placing the stitching about 1/4" from the edge of the second piece, and again 1/4" in from that. Add a row of zigzag

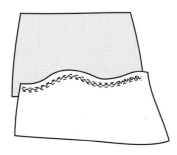

between the two rows of stitching.

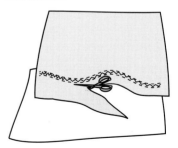

Note: This stitching may be done in other ways, such as with machine embroidery using the decorative stitches found on many sewing machines.

4. Turn the piece over and cut away the excess fabric, leaving at least a 1/4" seam allowance on the back. If the cut-away piece is sufficiently large, save it to add back onto the block.

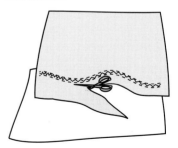

5. Continue to add patches following Steps 2-4. As the block grows, shape it into a 29" x 22" rectangle. (By placing the block on a large cutting mat, you can easily see its dimensions and whether the sides are straight.)

Repeat instructions 2 through 5 to make the required number of blocks.

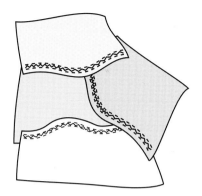

Below: Seam finishes on the reverse side of the throw.

6. Machine-wash the blocks and line or tumble dry (wash and dry the same as you would blue jeans). With scissors, trim away the denim threads that have worked loose along the patch seams. Leave fringes or seam allowances of 1/4"; do not trim right up to the stitching.

7. Embellish the blocks as desired. You can couch on meandering trims, shape ribbons into bows and zigzag them on, and add appliqués. Cut out leaf shapes from the green velveteen and sew them alongside the Broderie Perse florals, zigzagging the edges. Consult Part 2 for instructions.

Finishing the Throw

1. With right sides together, sew the long edges of the rectangles together to form two columns (see diagram on page 49), each of three blocks, using a 1/2" seam allowance. Press the seams open. With right sides together, sew the two columns together and press.

2. To keep the seam allowances open and flat, machine-couch a braid, cable, or other trim, meandering it over the seams. Check that seam allowances stay flat as you sew.

3. Cut the eyelet into four lengths, each one-and-a-half times the length of each side of the throw. Join the lengths, folding and sewing a miter at each corner. Trim, then zigzag over, the seam just sewn.

4. Run a gathering thread 1/4" from the top of the eyelet. Pin the eyelet to the quilt

with right sides together, gathering it to fit the quilt top and aligning the miters with the corners. Sew along the gathering line. Finish by zigzagging or overcasting the seam.

Creative Notes

The exotic form of a day lily can be the inspiration for embroidery or appliqué.

• This throw can be personalized by adding hand, machine, or silk ribbon embroidery, acrylic paintings (heat-set before washing: cover painting with a cloth and press with an iron at wool setting for about 20 seconds), and other washable techniques. Use the quilt blocks as canvases for creative fun!

Intermediate

Bullions & Battenberg Wool Quilt

Wool is a lofty, springy fiber that is a joy to work with. Although wool fabrics seem to adore the addition of cotton laces and other trims machine sewn onto them, and readily accept pearl cotton straight stitched by machine along seams, they are equally wonderful for hand embroidery. Wool is an exceptionally easy fiber to embroider, so it is an excellent material for novices.

The Battenberg cocktail napkins used in this quilt are a set of eight gracefully aged heirloom linens that now provide perfect offsets to the embroidered crazy blocks. They are lightly held in place with a round of pearl cotton machine stitching and hand tacked with French Knot and Bullion Stitch posies worked in wool.

The method used for the wool quilt shown here is a variation of Topstitch Appliqué. To reduce bulk, the patch edges are not turned under, but are zigzagged by machine, then concealed under trims and laces.

Size: 50" square (15" square blocks), not including the lace edging.

Frothy white flowers are the garden's lace.

At home with old roses, the Bullions & Battenberg wool quilt features a hand-crocheted edging.

Palette

Patch colors include pure reds, mossy greens, and whites with black, gold, and cream.

Thread colors include rose, pale green, light blue, bright pink, yellow, and red.

Materials

- 1-1/2 yards of 60" wide red wool fabric
- Scraps or small pieces of fabrics, including wool suitings and other wool types in above colors, mostly plain with some plaids or stripes (the moss green used here is a cotton flannel)
- 3-1/2 yards of 44" wide muslin
- 3-1/2 yards of 44" wide cotton backing fabric
- 3/8" or wider cotton laces, ribbons, gimpe, and braid trims for Topstitch Appliqué
- Size 50 100-percent cotton sewing threads to match Topstitch Appliqué trims
- Persian embroidery wool in the colors listed above, red for ties
- Size 8 pearl cotton in the colors listed above
- Eight linen cocktail napkins, 8" to 9-1/2" square (other items may be substituted, such as crocheted doilies or hankies, round or square)
- 6-3/4 yards of purchased or handmade lace, about 2-1/4" wide

Note: Use 1/4" seam allowances for assembly.

Cutting

1. Cut the muslin and red wool into 15-1/2" squares to have 16 squares of muslin and eight of wool.

Making the Crazy Blocks

1. Work Topstitch Appliqué on eight of the muslin foundations, following the instructions on page 31, except overlap each patch only about 1/2" onto previous patches.

2. One patch at a time, zigzag the overlapping edge (or edges) of the patch. Place a trim over the zigzagging to conceal the stitching and straight-stitch along the edges of the trim with matching thread.

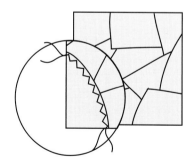

Tip: Begin with patches that have edges going under other patches and continue by finding and sewing the next most-underlapped patch. End with those patches that overlap all others.

3. Work machine Patch Seam Embroidery (see page 122), stitching pearl cotton along the seams of each block. Add embellishments according to the instructions in Part 2, such as trapunto and couched yarns. Make wool tassels according to the instructions below. If desired, use one strand of Persian wool to hand-embroider floral embroideries and bumblebees using the Bullion Stitch (see page 138).

Wool Tassels

The following method is for making tassels that are machine-sewn to a patched block. Choose a length of yarn that will make a tassel the thickness and length desired. Use thread that matches the yarn and place the patched block under the sewing machine needle where the tassel will be sewn.

1. Wind the yarn around four fingers and grasp it tightly at the center.

2. Using a short zigzag machine stitch, place the looped yarn next to the machine needle, pulling it snug to the needle. Stitch several times over the yarn, adjusting the stitch to land on either side.

3. Fold the upper half down and machine-tack below the first tack. Cut the loose ends of yarn straight across.

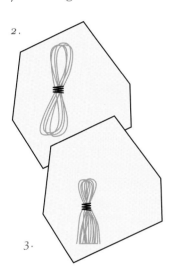

French Knot for a tiny rose (see page 140) and two Bullion stitches for leaves for each motif (see page 138).

Finishing the Quilt

1. Following the diagram, sew the blocks into columns of four. Sew the columns together.

2. Add a knife-edge backing (see page 134), then invisibly hand-stitch the lace to the seam. Use red yarn to tie the quilt (see page 135), having the ties on the right side.

Making the Red Blocks

1. Center a linen napkin diagonally on each of the eight red blocks. Baste each in place. Freehand machine-stitch pearl cotton, meandering around the edges of the napkin. Hand-embroider small floral motifs. Work a

Creative Notes

• Increase the number of blocks to make a warm and cozy winter bed quilt.
• Although red makes a dramatic statement, another color may be substituted. Try picturing this design with fawn brown as the dominant color, to be used as a wintertime couch throw.

Some plants add texture to the garden just like some fabrics add texture to the crazy quilt.

Method 3: Confetti Piecing

Confetti Piecing is a way to make "crazy" pieced quilts using cotton fabrics. Foundations, embroidery, embellishments, templates, and patterns are not used; you simply cut, sew, and press. It has to be the quickest and easiest form of piecing ever, yet the results give the impression of complex piecing.

The faceted effects of Confetti Piecing are like sun-dappled garden subjects.

Get to know the method by working up a sample in fabric; it's very easy to learn. After doing several cuts (followed by a "sew" for each), you'll have it. It takes a lot of explaining, as you can see by the instructions on the following page, but the actual process is very simple. If you have done geometric piecing with templates or a rotary cutter, you may find this a freeing and satisfying method. I find

it a pleasure to sew a Confetti quilt after doing many hours of handwork on my other crazy quilts.

A rotary cutter, cutting mat (at least 24" x 36"), and an acrylic ruler for use with rotary cutters are recommended for Confetti piecing. If you don't have this equipment, fabric shears can be used instead, with a yardstick and pencil or tailor's chalk to mark the cutting lines. For the piec-

ing, use a quality, all-purpose 100-percent cotton sewing thread in a shade that blends with the fabrics.

If machine or hand embroidery will be worked on the quilt, add a muslin foundation after the piecing is completed. An embroidered and embellished quilt of fancy fabrics can be made using this method, although the individual pieces should be kept large to avoid excessive seaming and allow space for embellishments.

Instructions for Confetti Piecing

Note: Use a 1/4" seam allowance throughout.

Tools needed

- Rotary cutter
- Acrylic ruler for use with a rotary cutter
- 24" x 36" cutting mat
- Steam iron and ironing board
- Sewing machine

1. Select eight 44"-45" wide cotton fabrics in a mix of prints and solids. Choose from quilting cottons, adding broadcloth, sateen, flannel, or other lightweight wovens as desired. Stack the fabrics evenly. For 1/4 yard lengths, cut 4-1/2" pieces for 4-1/2" x 9" cuts. For 1/2 yard lengths, stack them the same and cut 9" pieces for 9" x 18" cuts.

2. Select two of the colors and sew them together to make an approximate square. Select another two colors and sew onto each end of the square. Press the seams to one side after each is sewn. Repeat to make a second block using the four remaining colors.

3. Cut one of the two blocks diagonally. Take one of the pieces, place it right side together onto the uncut block and cut along the previously

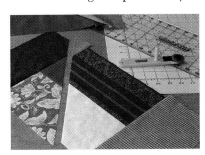

cut edge. Set the cut-off piece aside, then sew a seam along the diagonal edge. Open out and press the seam to one side, using steam. Match the diagonal edges of the remaining two cut pieces, and having right sides together, sew them and press open. Continue to cut, sew, and press. You choose where to make the cuts. The cut and sew process can be continued until most

of the pieces are very small. The finer the confetti pieces, the more seams there will be, and the more fabric is used.

4. Repeat Steps 2 and 3 and, at some point, sew the pieces into a block and square off the edges. Make the block the size required for the quilt you wish to make and continue to make blocks until you have the number needed.

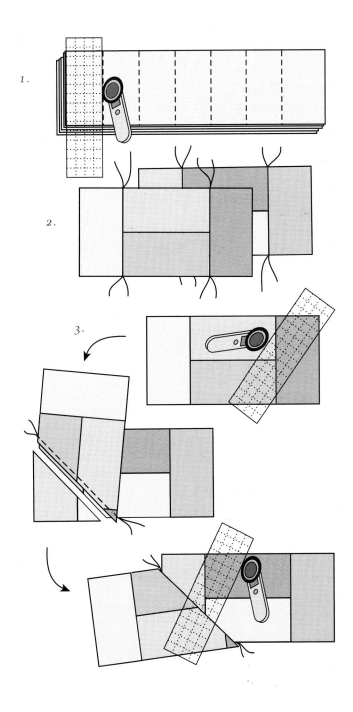

1.

2.

3.

Colorplay

Confetti piecing appears as facetting: this quilt almost sparkles as if flashes of light and depths of shade were dancing on its surface. Add a lofty batting and tie the quilt to make a fluffy bedcover that will be wonderful to snuggle under; I've always adored tied quilts for their fluffy comforter-ness. This quilt was made twin bed-size, but you can make a larger size by adding extra blocks.

Created in an analogous color scheme, several colors that fall next to each other on a color wheel are used for this quilt. Lighter squares alternate with darker ones, resulting in a soft checkerboard effect.

Size: 64-1/2" x 72" (56 7-1/2" blocks and 6" borders). The actual finished size may differ due to batting and tying.

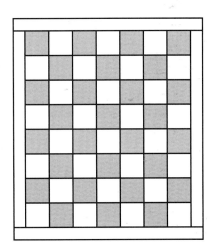

Colorplay poses with lilacs in the spring garden.

Palette

Rich teals, blues, and purples, analogous hues, are offset by alternating blocks of the same in lighter shades. Two fabrics, a white and an off-white, are white-on-white prints.

Materials

(All fabrics 100-percent cotton, 44" wide)

- 1/2 yard lengths of eight cotton fabrics, a mix of prints and solids in medium to dark shades of teal, blue, and purple
- 1/2 yard lengths of eight cotton fabrics, a mix of prints and solids in light to pale shades of the teal, blue, and purple, including white and off-white
- 65" x 73" lofty polyester batting
- 4 yards of plain or printed cotton backing fabric
- 2-1/2 yards of border fabric, the same as one of the prints
- 7-1/2 yards purchased or self-made 1/2" wide bias binding
- 1 spool of size 8 pearl cotton, any blending color
- 100-percent cotton sewing thread to blend with the fabrics

Note: Use 1/4" seam allowances throughout.

Cutting

1. Cut four border strips, two 6-1/2" x 60-1/2" for the sides and two 6-1/2" x 65" for the top and bottom, from the border fabric.

2. Cut and sew the backing fabric to make one piece 65" wide x 72-1/2" long.

Making the Quilt Top

1. Using eight darker fabrics, follow the instructions on page 57 to work Confetti Piecing. Make 28 blocks, each 8" square. Set the blocks aside.

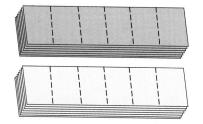

2. Repeat Step 1, using the lighter colors to make 28 blocks, each 8" square.

3. Alternating a light block with a dark one, sew them into columns according to the diagram (on page 59). Steampress the seams to one side. Sew the columns together and press the seams.

Finishing the Quilt

1. Sew on the side borders, then the top and bottom. Add the batting and backing and then bind the quilt (see page 134). Tie the quilt using pearl cotton, placing ties at the intersections and in the centers of the blocks and evenly along the border.

The interesting shades seen in a tidal pool could be a quilt design in the making.

Creative Notes

• There are many variations that can be done on this theme. Shift the analogous color scheme to yellows and oranges to suggest a sunrise or sunset, or shades of greens and blue-greens to give the feeling of a forest.

• The quilt can be quilted in the traditional manner rather than tied. Use a low-loft batting, the quilting pattern of your choice, and quilt by hand or machine.

Easy

Summer Breeze

The mellow colors and soft florals of this quilt make it a cool throw for the sun porch. The flowery shapes of the yo-yos seem to add a feminine touch while providing both texture and visual interest, as do the soft creamy yellows that are the basis of the color scheme. Much of the fun of making this quilt lies in accumulating a basketful of stitched yo-yos. I always try to have a project on hand that requires little thought and can be done anywhere—making yo-yos is perfect!

Although the yo-yos take some time to prepare, the Confetti blocks go together in a snap. Because no batting is used, a foundation of muslin is added to the blocks in this quilt. White eyelet lace is added into some of the seams, and as a finishing touch, the blocks are topstitched.

Size: 52" square (25 8" blocks; the yo-yos are 2" in diameter).

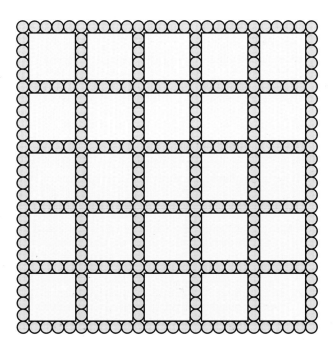

Summer Breeze is a perfect throw for summer lounging.

Palette

This quilt includes a soft floral with a yellow background, a floral print with a cream background, and a small floral print that is also used for the yo-yos. Solids are a yellow cotton flannel, teal, turquoise, coral, and medium blue.

Materials

(All fabrics 100-percent cotton, 44" wide)
- 4 yards of a floral quilting cotton
- 1/4 yard each of eight different printed and plain cotton fabrics, including a cotton flannel
- Several yards of white eyelet lace, 2" to 4" wide
- 1-3/4 yards of a print or solid cotton backing fabric
- 1-3/4 yards of muslin
- 100-percent cotton sewing thread to blend with the fabrics
- YLI 100-percent Cotton Quilting or YLI Select Thread in 006, yellow
- Tracing paper, pencil, and scissors

Note: Use 1/4" seam allowances throughout.

Cutting

1. Trace and cut out the Yo-yo Pattern. Cut 276 yo-yos out of the 4 yards of floral cotton. (The fabric can be folded in order to cut several at once.)
2. Cut the backing fabric and the muslin each into 25 squares, each 8-1/2".

Making the Quilt

1. Following the instructions on page 57, work Confetti Piecing to make 25 blocks, each 8-1/2" square, adding the eyelet lace into some of the first seams sewn.
2. Add a muslin square to the back of each block, pin, and baste around outer edges.
3. Machine topstitch around some of the patches with the yellow quilting thread.
4. Place a backing square right side together with each block and sew around, leaving an opening to turn. Turn, press, and slipstitch the opening closed.
5. Make 276 yo-yos as follows: Press under 1/4" of the outer edge of each fabric circle. Hand-baste around the pressed edge, pull up on the thread to

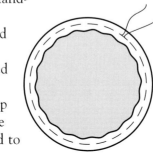

gather, and fasten off with several tiny stitches. Flatten, centering the opening.
6. To stitch the yo-yos together, thread a needle with the yellow thread. Holding two yo-yos right sides together, fasten the thread to one yo-yo with several tiny stitches placed close together, then stitch the yo-yos together, keeping the stitches small. Fasten off with several tiny stitches.
7. Stitch four yo-yos together, then stitch them along one side of a block. Stitch another block to the opposite sides of the same yo-yos. Continue adding yo-yos and blocks to make a row of five blocks with yo-yo spacers. Make five of these and join them with rows of yo-yos. Add yo-yos around the quilt, including the four corners.

Creative Notes

• The time and care that goes into this quilt make it suitable for an heirloom. Try it in soft off-whites and delicate prints for a future bride.

The ethereal forms of Siberian Iris make a statement along a pathway.

Summer Breeze
Yo-yo Pattern

1/4" seam allowance included

Challenging

Just Dollin' Around

What child wouldn't be delighted to have a quilt bordered by dolls? Dolls in the style of cut-outs happily join hands around this cotton twin bed-size quilt. Buttons and bows on the dolls are optional (leave them off for a very young child). With the cowboy option, this quilt can be made for a girl or a boy. The dolls are easy to piece accurately using a foundation method.

By backing the dolls with a smooth white cotton fabric, this becomes an autograph quilt. Use permanent fabric markers to have the child's friends each sign the back of a doll. Heat-set the signatures by pressing with an iron on wool setting for 20 seconds on the fabric, being careful not to scorch.

Size: 62-1/2" x by 93" long. (8 blocks, each 21-1/4" x 20-3/4", 1-1/2" wide sashings, and 8-1/2" wide doll border consists of 33 dolls).

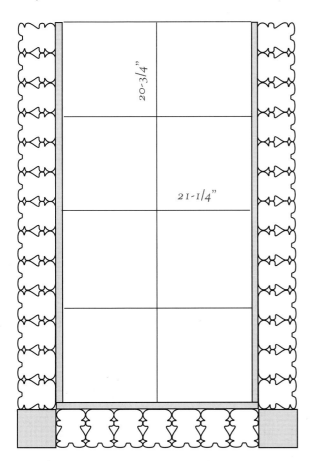

Palette

The quilt shown consists of soft to medium shades of peach, rose, green, white, and turquoise in prints and solids. For the cowboy quilt, choose a color scheme such as blues, browns, and greens.

Materials

(All fabrics 100-percent cotton, 44" wide)
- 1/2 yard each of eight different prints and solids
- Several yards of 1" to 4" wide cotton eyelet laces in white (for doll quilt) for sewing into seams of Confetti Piecing
- 5 yards of turquoise fabric for sashings and backing
- 46" x 85" cotton poly batting that can be tied up to 8" apart

A gnarled old apple tree extends a branch for Just Dollin' Around.

Note: Because the hair, face, and hand colors can be adapted as desired to reflect children of different ethnicities, specific colors are not given below. Choose your preferred colors for each.

Materials for the Dolls [Changes for the cowboys are indicated by brackets]

- 3/4 yard each of two different prints for doll dresses
- 3/4 yard for hair [hat]
- [3/4 yard for chaps]
- [1/2 yard for cowboy shirt]
- 1/4 yard for faces and hands
- 1/4 yard for feet [boots]
- 1-1/2 yards of 44" wide fabric for doll backings in a color that blends with dress [shirt] colors
- 2-1/2 yards of 34" wide cotton craft batting
- 1/8" wide ribbon and buttons for optional trimmings
- 100-percent cotton sewing thread for hair [hat], zigzag topstitching, and a color to blend with fabrics
- One spool of size 8 pearl cotton in your choice of color for tying the quilt
- Tracing paper, pencil, scissors

Note: Use 1/4" seam allowances throughout.

Cutting

1. Trace and cut out the pattern pieces. Cut doll

[cowboy] fabrics for 33 dolls. Cut 16 of the doll dresses of one print and 17 of the other. Cut out a backing and cotton craft batting for each doll [cowboy].

2. Cut 9" squares, two each of: doll's dress [shirt] fabric, craft batting, and backing fabric.

3. From the turquoise fabric, cut two side sashings, each 2" x 83-1/2", and one bottom sashing 2" x 46".

4. Cut and sew the turquoise fabric to make a backing 46" x 85".

Notes:
- From here on, the word "doll" refers to either the doll or the cowboy.
- Accurate seam allowances are required for fitting the dolls to the quilt dimensions.
- To save time, use assembly-line sewing of the dolls. Do each step for all of the dolls before continuing to the next step. (But assemble one doll first so you understand the process.)

Making the Dolls

Appliqué Technique for Sewing on the Face, Hands, and Feet

1. Overlap the pieces to be joined with right sides facing up and seamlines aligned. Machine-stitch along the

seamline. Trim the seam allowance of the topmost fabric close to the stitching. Machine-zigzag to cover the cut edge and the seam.

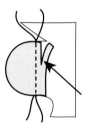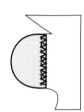

2. Center the face onto the hair [hat] and appliqué as in Step 1. Turn the piece upside down and carefully cut away the area of hair [hat] behind the face, cutting next to the stitching. Be very careful not to cut the face. Set aside.

3. Lay a dress on a cotton batting piece, aligning edges. [For the cowboy, place the chaps and shirt on the batting and appliqué to join at the waist.] Appliqué hands and feet onto the doll as in Step 1.

4. With right sides together, sew on the face/hair [hat] piece along the seam line. Open out and press. Do zigzag stitching as indicated on the pattern to delineate the lines of the hair [hat].

5. Place a backing piece right sides together on the doll and sew around, leaving the top of the head open for turning. Trim and clip the seams carefully, turn right side out, and press.

6. Dolls are joined to each other at four places: hair, hands, dress [chaps], and feet. **Either** do a narrow zigzag to attach these points, **or** invisibly hand stitch. Join 13 for each side border, and seven for the end.

7. To make two corner blocks, place the 9" squares of fabric and backing right sides together, add batting, and sew around, leaving an opening to turn. Turn, press, and sew the opening closed. The same as in Step 6, attach the dolls to the corners (see diagram on page 67).

Making the Confetti Blocks

1. Following the instructions on pages 57, work Confetti Piecing to make eight blocks, each 21-3/4" x 21-1/4". Sew them together according to the diagram on page 67, then sew on the two side sashings, followed by the bottom edge sashing.

Finish the Quilt

1. Place doll borders with right sides together along the edges of the sashings, pin, and sew along the seamline of the heads to attach the dolls to the sashing.

2. Lay the batting onto the wrong side of the quilt top and trim even with the seam allowance to which the dolls are sewn. Add the backing, baste, then fold in the seam allowances of both the backing and sashing. By hand, slipstitch the seam closed. Instead of slipstitching at the top edge of the quilt, you may instead add a binding (see page 134). Tie the quilt using pearl cotton (see page 135).

3. Finish the dolls by adding any desired details such as buttons with a bow on the doll's dress, or buttons on the cowboy's chaps (see photos). The bows are tied and then sewn on by machine using short tacking stitches. Do not add these details if the quilt is for a very young child.

This little guy observes the photo shoot while savoring a strawberry.

Creative Notes

• Design your own border by making shapes such as bunnies, teddy bears, trees, or stars. Make each shape into a separate unit, adding seam allowances, and assemble like the dolls above.

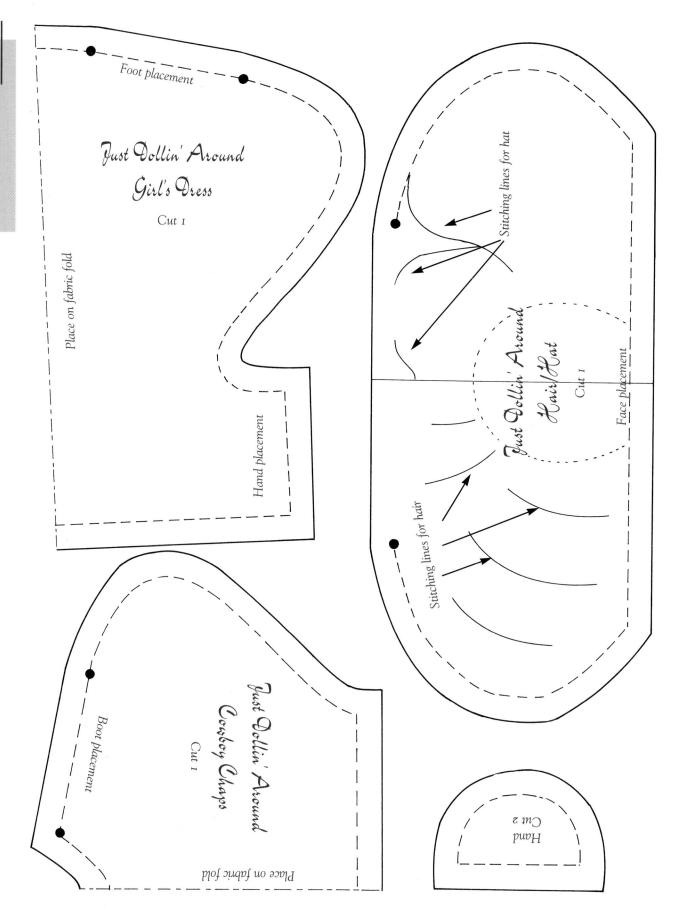

Foot placement

Just Dollin' Around

Girl's Dress

Cut 1

Place on fabric fold

Hand placement

Stitching lines for hat

Just Dollin' Around

Hair/Hat

Cut 1

Face placement

Stitching lines for hair

Just Dollin' Around

Cowboy Chaps

Cut 1

Boot placement

Place on fabric fold

Hand

Cut 2

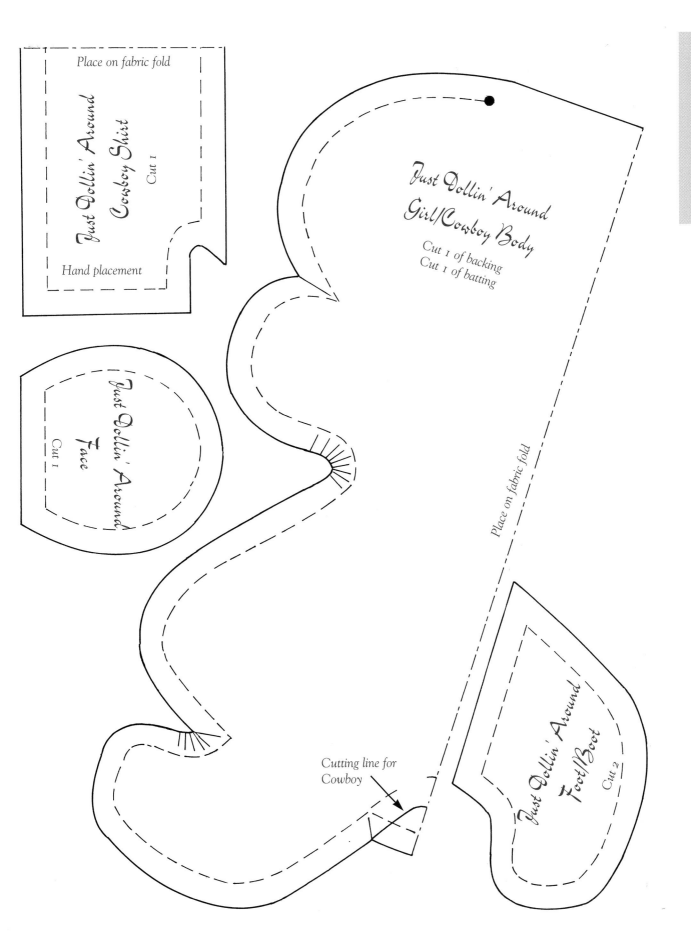

Place on fabric fold

Just Dollin' Around
Cowboy Shirt
Cut 1

Hand placement

Just Dollin' Around
Girl/Cowboy Body
Cut 1 of backing
Cut 1 of batting

Just Dollin' Around
Face
Cut 1

Place on fabric fold

Just Dollin' Around
Foot/Boot
Cut 2

Cutting line for
Cowboy

A country-style setting serves The Maine Blues Table Topper well.

Maine Blues Table Topper

Blue sky, blue ocean, and blue hills in the distance are characteristics of Maine, a beautiful state and a favorite vacation spot for many. This table topper features fabrics in crisp shades of blue alongside pristine white and a "shark tooth" (or, more appropriately, "lobster tooth") edging. The top is made as a whole-quilt. Another way to make a similar topper is to divide the top into blocks. Make the quilt the size of your table (see below). No foundation or batting is used for the table topper.

Size: The quilt shown is 48" x 53", not including the 46-tooth edging. Measure your table top, then add about 18" to the length and width for a 9" drop. To fit a round table, make the topper square-shaped, adding about 18" to the square for a 9" drop at the sides (the corners will hang lower).

Palette

The fabrics used include prints in shades of blue from light to navy, stripes, and florals. The white fabric is a white-on-white print.

Materials

(All fabrics 100-percent cotton, 44" wide)
(Yardages given are for the 48" x 53" topper. Purchase additional 1/2-yard lengths to make a larger topper.)

- 1/2 yard each of six different printed cotton fabrics
- 1-1/2 yards of white cotton fabric (reserve 1/2 yard for the shark tooth edging)
- 1/4 yard of a medium blue soft print for the sashings
- 3 yards of white or pale blue backing fabric
- 100-percent cotton sewing thread to blend with fabrics
- YLI 100-percent Cotton Quilting or YLI Select Thread in white or light blue
- Tracing paper, pencil, scissors

Note: Use 1/4" seam allowances throughout.

Exuberant wild flowers at the beach.

Making the Confetti Top

1. Stack the 1/2 yard pieces of fabric. Cut 1 yard of the white into two pieces, each 18" x 44", and add to the stack. Follow the instructions for Confetti Piecing (see page 57). Cut and sew the Confetti sections into one piece in the size needed for your table (see diagram on page 73).

Finishing the Topper

1. Out of the medium blue, cut two sashing strips, each 1-1/4" wide by the length of the topper. Sew one to each side. Now, cut two, each 1-1/4" wide by the total width of the topper. Sew to the top and bottom edges. Press seams toward the sashing.

2. Trace and cut out the "shark tooth" pattern. For each point needed, cut two of white fabric. With right sides together, sew along the diagonal sides of each pair, leaving the straight edge open. Trim, turn, and press. With right sides together, pin the teeth along the sashing, keeping them inside the seam allowances at the ends of the sashings. Machine baste.

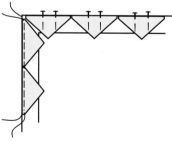

3. Cut and sew the pale blue backing fabric to fit to the raw edges of the topper, piec-

A classic Maine lighthouse scene.

ing the fabric if necessary. With right sides together, sew the backing on through all layers, leaving an opening to turn. Turn right side out, press, and slipstitch the opening closed.

4. Baste across the topper several times, then quilt the topper by machine stitching in the ditch along some of the seams (enough to hold the layers in place) using quilting thread (see page 135).

Rolling Maine hills.

Creative Notes

• This project is a great, quick gift idea suitable for many occasions. Try making it in shades of rose and greens for a romantic table covering, or yellows to brighten up a room. Use plenty of white for a pristine, crisp-clean look.

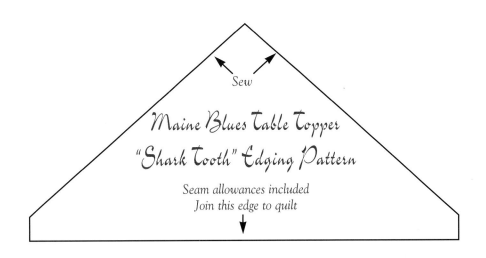

Sew

Maine Blues Table Topper
"Shark Tooth" Edging Pattern

Seam allowances included
Join this edge to quilt

Above: Draped across beach stones, Oceanic Greens is ready for a picnic.

Easy

Oceanic Greens Table Topper

Cool greens with crisp whites remind me of ocean waves lapping onto the shore. Use the instructions for Maine Blues on page 74, choosing cool, oceanic green colors in place of blues. Make the topper the size needed for your table.

Looking out to sea on a misty day.

Southwestern Flair Appliqué Quilt

Confetti sashings and bold appliqués are combined in a bed quilt that is sure to be a focal point in any bedroom. Baskets in zesty southwestern colors add graphic intensity in this blending of traditional and crazy quilting styles. Aptly demonstrated here is the Confetti method's versatility when combining it with other flat-surface techniques. The faceted Confetti provides a visual counterpoint to the curving lines of the appliqués in this quilt.

The floral basket design is drawn from my memory of some brittle, aged wallpaper I saw while exploring a deserted Midwestern farmhouse. The design was a representation of an appliqué quilt with simple piecing between the blocks. I waited many years for an opportunity to use the design and have significantly adapted it for this quilt.

Size: 92-1/2" x 102-1/2" (12 17-1/2" square appliqué blocks, 4-1/2" wide sashings, and 10" wide borders to fit a full-size bed).

Above: Yellow lilies inspired the florals in this quilt
Left: Southwestern Flair draped across an antique bed.

Palette

The colors used in this quilt include turquoise with rusts, yellows, and sage, in solids for the appliqués, and a few prints added to them for the Confetti sections. One of the prints was used for the quilt's snazzy self-made binding.

Materials

(All fabrics 100-percent cotton, 44" wide)
- 6-1/4 yards of turquoise cotton fabric
- 1/4 yard each of 8 fabrics for Confetti
- Size 50 100-percent cotton sewing threads to match appliqué fabrics (see below)
- 93" x 103" lofty polyester batting
- 6 yards of cotton backing fabric in your choice of color
- 12 yards of purchased or self-made 1-1/2" bias binding
- Size 8 pearl cotton in yellow, rust, and turquoise
- Artist's tracing paper, pencil, scissors
- Lightweight cardboard, chalk pencil for making the appliqués

Fabrics for Appliqués

(All fabrics 100-percent cotton, 44" wide)
- 1 yard each of rust and dark red
- 1/2 yard each of light and dark yellow
- 1-1/2 yards of sage green

Note: Use 1/4" seam allowances throughout.

Cutting

1. Out of turquoise fabric, cut 12 squares, each 18", two outer borders, each 10-1/2" x 103", and a bottom border, 10-1/2" x 71".
2. Trace and cut out the basket patterns and cut the fabrics as indicated on the pattern pieces (follow instructions below for cutting the remaining appliqué pieces).

Colors for the Appliqué Blocks

For six of the blocks, use dark red as the main basket color, light yellow for the large flower, and dark yellow for the smaller flowers. For the remaining six blocks, use rust as the main basket color, dark yellow for the large flower, and light yellow for the smaller flowers.

Making the Appliqué Blocks

1. Machine-sew the basket pieces into rows, then sew the rows together. When sewing on the triangles at the bottom of the basket, do

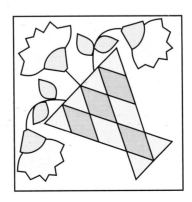

not sew into the upper seam allowances of these pieces so they can be pressed to the back. Press all seams to one side. Press the basket edges under 1/4" all around.
2. Follow this method for cutting and pressing the remaining appliqués: Trace the pattern pieces onto tracing paper, then glue to cardboard and cut them out. Lay the cardboard onto the fabric and trace around with a chalk pencil, adding a 1/4" seam allowance. Cut out the piece. Lay the cardboard onto the reverse side of the appliqué, and fold the seam allowance onto the cardboard and press.

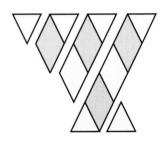

3. To accurately place the basket on each of the 18" turquoise squares, first fold the square diagonally and lightly finger-press, leaving a slight crease. Center the basket along the crease. The bottom of the basket should be placed exactly 4-1/4" from the raw edge of the block. Place the remaining appliqués according to the diagram and pin.
4. Using matching thread, slipstitch each appliqué in place.

Making the Quilt Top

1. Following the instructions on page 57, work Confetti piecing to make nine spacers, each 5" x 18", two sashings, each 5" x 84", two inner borders for top and bottom, each 5" x 62", and two inner borders for sides, each 5" x 93"

Finishing the Quilt

1. Arrange the appliqué blocks in alternating directions and colors and sew together (with right sides together) with the Confetti spacers and 5" x 84" sashings. Add the top and bottom inner Confetti borders, then the two side inner borders. Add the turquoise borders, first the bottom, and then the two side borders.

2. Arrange the appliqué pieces along the border and slipstitch. If desired, cut the bottom corners of the border into a rounded shape.

3. Cut and sew the backing fabric to make one piece 93" wide by 103" long. Stack the quilt top, batting, and backing with wrong sides together and baste. Work Running Stitch (see page 140) by hand in yellow pearl cotton just inside the outer edge of each block and around the inner edges of the border. Hand-tie the quilt (see page 135) throughout the appliqué blocks, along the spacers, sashings, and the border, using colors of pearl cotton that match or blend. Add the binding (see page 134).

Creative Notes

• When designing a quilt, I first sketch the design that is in my mind, often generating several variations of it. For Southwestern Flair, I made a trial appliqué block and a section of Confetti. Placing them side by side, along with the final sketch, it all looked fine, including the colors, balance, and composition (those things required to please the eye), so I went ahead and made the quilt. You may like to try this process to devise a quilt design of your own; the design opportunities for combining Confetti and appliqué are endless.

Lavender and the Maiden's Blush rose are cottage garden companions.

Southwestern Flair Straight Stem

Make 1 of sage green for each block
Make 2 of sage green for border

Southwestern Flair Basket

Cut 6 of rust for 6 of the blocks
Cut 6 of dark red for the remaining 6 blocks

Seam allowances included

Southwestern Flair Leaf

Make 4 of sage green for each block
Make 48 of sage green for border

Note: Dark and light colors are reversed for 6 of the baskets.

Southwestern Flair Basket

Cut 4 of rust
Cut 2 of dark red for 6 of the blocks

Cut 2 of rust
Cut 4 of dark red for the remaining 6 blocks

Seam allowances included

Southwestern Flair Flower Calyx

Make 3 of sage green for each block
Make 24 of sage green for border

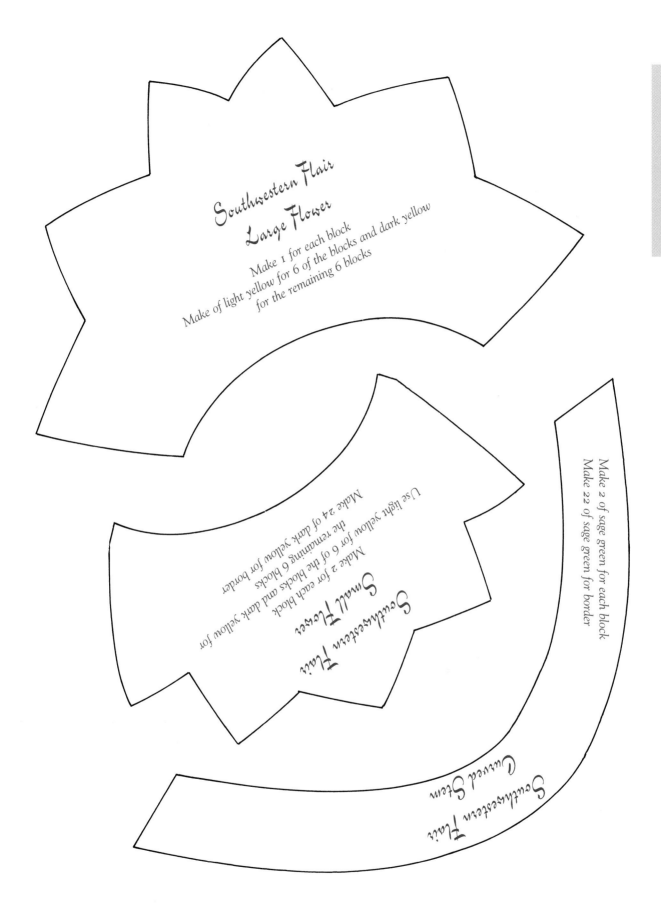

Southwestern Flair
Large Flower

Make 1 for each block
Make of light yellow for 6 of the blocks and dark yellow
for the remaining 6 blocks

Southwestern Flair
Small Flower

Make 2 for each block and dark yellow for
the remaining 6 blocks
Use light yellow for 6 of the blocks
Make 24 of dark yellow for border

Southwestern Flair
Curved Stem

Make 2 of sage green for each block
Make 22 of sage green for border

Challenging

$\mathcal{S}unrise\ \mathcal{R}eflections$

The Confetti method is ideal for creating "values" quilts, wherein one color fades from its deepest shades to its very palest. In this quilt, I used this principle to combine purple into yellow diagonally across the quilt. This idea can be varied by placing the blocks in different arrangements.

This quilt is machine quilted in a traditional manner. The quilting seems to further the refraction effect of the Confetti Piecing. It is done on the diagonal, opposing the directions created by the square blocks. Along the border, the stitching again runs counter to the strip-piecing.

Size: 50-1/2" square (25 9" blocks and 2-3/4" borders). The actual finished size may differ due to the batting and quilting.

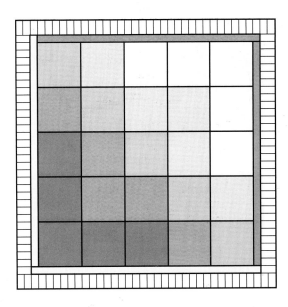

Sunrise Reflections in the misty spring garden.

Palette

This quilt includes shades of dusty violet and soft yellow-golds. Soft greens act like a neutral color in some of the prints, enhanced by a light moss-green thread used for the quilting.

Materials

(All fabrics 100-percent cotton, 44" wide)

- 1/2 yard each of eight different printed quilting cottons in dark to medium shades of dusty violet
- 1/2 yard each of eight different printed quilting cottons in deep to pastel shades of soft yellows and yellow-golds
- 52" square of cotton or low-loft polyester batting
- 3 yards of cotton backing fabric in any blending color
- 100-percent cotton sewing thread to blend with the fabric colors
- YLI 100-percent Cotton Quilting Thread in 009 Spring Green
- 100-percent cotton sewing thread to match the quilt backing (or use monofilament) for the bobbin thread while quilting
- 1/2" wide masking tape

Note: Use 1/4" seam allowances throughout.

Making the Quilt Top

1. Stack the eight yellow fabrics and cut them lengthwise for two 9" x 44" strips. Do the same with the purples. Follow the Confetti instructions on page 57 to make the blocks as follows: Cut a 4-1/2" section of the stacked yellows, work Confetti piecing, and set aside. Repeat until there is enough to make five blocks, each 9-1/2" square. Cut out the five blocks and set aside. Do the same with the purples and set aside.

2. Steps 2-4 begin to mix the colors. Keep the stacks of finished blocks in separate stacks. Restack the fabrics for six pieces of the yellows and two of the purples. Cut a 4-1/2" section of the stacked fabrics (repeating as necessary) and make five blocks. Stack them and set aside.

3. Restack the fabrics again for four pieces of the yellows and four of the purples. Make five blocks. Stack them and set aside.

4. Restack once again for two pieces of the yellows and six of the purples. Make five blocks and set aside.

Assemble the Quilt

1. Arrange the blocks in the order shown in the diagram (on page 85) and sew them together, first into columns, then sewing the columns together. Make sashings and the border as follows:

a. To make the inner borders: Out of the remaining fabrics, select one of the purple fabrics. Cut 3/4" wide strips, sewing them together lengthwise to make two strips. Sew one to one side of the quilt and the other to the top of the quilt (along the yellowist of the blocks). Repeat, making strips from one of the yellow fabrics and sewing these to the remaining sides of the quilt.

b. To make the outer borders: Stack the remaining fabrics into one stack of purples and one of yellows. Cut them into strips, each 2-1/4" long x 3/4" wide. Sew them together along the long edges, joining five or six purples, followed by five or six yellows, repeating this sequence. Make two borders 2-1/4" by the length of the quilt and sew them to opposite sides. Repeat to make two more that are slightly longer to fit the top and bottom of the quilt.

2. To make bindings for the quilt: Cut strips 1-1/2" wide by any length and join the short ends in any sequence until there is sufficient length to go around the quilt. Set these aside.

3. Prepare the quilt layers for machine quilting (see pages 134 and 135).

4. Place masking tape on the quilt top to mark the first line of quilting diagonally across the quilt and precisely along the joins of the blocks, from corner to corner. Stitch along one edge of the tape up to the inner borders and remove the tape. Continue to mark and quilt along the joins of the blocks. Next, place the tape so the stitching lines will be exactly in the middles of the previous lines. Continue to divide the space until quilting lines are 1-1/2" apart. Repeat

to quilt diagonally in the opposite direction. (Always remove tape right after stitching and do not place it unless you will be stitching right away.)

5. Quilt along the inner borders by stitching in the ditch. Quilt three rows evenly spaced along each border, spacing the rows evenly apart. Bind the quilt (see page 134).

Creative Notes

• The creative possibilities here are many. Envision a quilt in rose and green prints diffusing into the blues and whites of sky, or earthy browns into forest greens.

Yet another of nature's glorious color schemes.

Method 4: Strip Patching

Strip Patching is a variation of the commonly known sew n' flip machine method of crazy patching, which often results in patches radiating from a central patch; it tends to resemble a version of Log Cabin patching gone awry. The challenges of sew n' flip include creating variation in patch sizes and shapes and in how to add patches as the work progresses.

Strip Patching is quicker and easier to do, beginning at the top of a foundation strip and proceeding to the bottom. There are fewer corners to back yourself into because the narrow format simplifies patch placement.

Begin by preparing a quantity of patches using the methods in Part 2. Make gathered and shaped-edge patches and work zigzag motifs and appliqués, medallions, created patches, and couched patches. Reserve patch seam embroidery, through-the-quilt methods, and ribbonworked florals until after the quilt is patched.

How to Do Strip Patching

Tools needed:
- Iron and ironing board
- Fabric shears
- Sewing machine

1. Begin with a strip of foundation fabric in the size needed for the quilt you are making. Cut a patch-sized piece of fabric and lay it at the top of the foundation. Cut another and place it right side together on the first and machine sew the seam, using a 1/4" seam allowance. Open out the second patch and press.

2. The third patch is applied the same way as the second. Sew the seam and press. Continue to add patches in this way. If desired, sew laces into some of the seams as patches are added.

3. Trim out any excessive seam allowances as patches

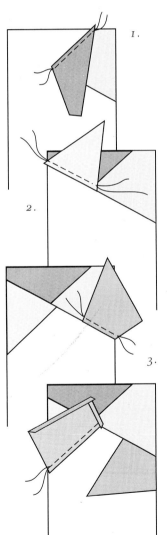

are added and sewn. Press under and pin any edges that cannot be sewn. These can be slipstitched or fastened with embroidery later. Trim patches even with the edges of the foundation.

4. If a gap occurs, simply add a patch to cover it.

Challenging

Midsummer Tango

The first name I chose for this wall quilt was "Midsummer's Tangle," but I changed it to "Tango" because it appears that the almost invasive tangling of stems is quite like a slow and purposeful dance. Riots of floriferous color and twining stems characterize a continually metamorphosing perennial garden. As if in a slow dance, stems and leaves intertwine in the grand tapestry of nature's weaving.

Stuffed appliqué gives dimension to this representation of a garden's small corner. A strip-patched inner border carries along the theme with ribbonwork floral motifs enclosed not by a picket fence, but by a twining stem and dark green outermost edging.

This design is considered "challenging" due to the complexity of its construction. Also, the appliqués are placed "freehand" without markings to follow.

Size: 54" square (22" square floral center, 10" wide inner borders (Strip Patched panels), and 6" wide outer borders).

Gracefully twining grapevines share a spot in the garden with Midsummer Tango.

Palette

A soft floral print fabric forms the basis of the patch colors. In this fabric are rust, teal, and brown on a rosy brown background. Two cotton velveteens in subtle brown prints add depth to the color scheme. To these colors, some purple, black, white, cream, gold, yellow, and blue were added.

Embroidery threads include shades of peach, rust, gold, blue, jade, beige, gray, and violet.

Materials

(All fabrics 44" wide)

- Assorted patch and appliqué fabrics, including the acetates: satin, moiré, and taffeta; and cotton velveteen in the colors listed above
- Small amount of stuffing
- 3/4 yard of white 100-percent cotton velveteen
- 1-1/4 yards of muslin
- Venice and other laces, trims, heirloom lace insertions, ribbons, silk ribbon for embroidery, etc.
- 5/8 yard of off-white bridal satin border fabric
- 1 yard of light green fabric for appliqués
- 3-1/4 yards of backing fabric in the color of your choice
- 5/8 yard of dark green bengaline fabric for quilt edging
- Several yards of 1/8" wide ribbons for tying the quilt
- Size 8 pearl cotton in the colors listed above
- One spool each of size 8 pearl cotton in light and medium peach
- Size 50 100-percent cotton sewing threads to match floral colors

Note: Use 1/4" seam allowances throughout.

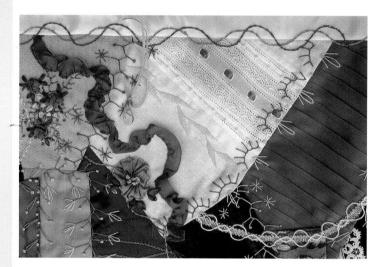

Cutting

1. Cut a 22-1/2" square each of white velveteen and muslin. Place the muslin on the back of the velveteen and handle the two as one.

2. Trace and cut out the appliqué pieces according to the patterns. Mix and match fabric types and colors to your liking. (Note: For velveteen flowers, use a backing of plain cotton to avoid adding bulk.) After making and pinning the stuffed appliqué flowers to the background fabric, out of green, cut bias strips 3/4" wide to make stems of sufficient length (see the photo below). Press under the stems' long edges.

3. For Strip Patching, cut four muslin foundations, two 10-1/2" x 22-1/2" and two 10-1/2" x 42-1/2".

4. Out of the off-white bridal satin, cut four borders, two 6-1/2" x 42-1/2" and two 6-1/2" x 54-1/2".

5. Cut and sew the backing fabric to make a 54-1/2" square.

6. For the quilt's outer edges, cut the dark green into four strips, each 5-1/2" x 56".

7. For the satin border appliqués, out of light green fabric, cut 24 leaves using the small leaf pattern. Press the edges of the leaves under. Cut 7/8" wide bias strips and sew them together to make a piece 6-1/2 yards long. Press under the strip's long edges to have the raw edges meeting in the center.

Making the Floral Center

1. For each stuffed appliqué, sew two pieces right sides together along the seamlines. Trim seams and clip curves. Most of the pieces are sewn completely around; for these, make a slash in the backing fabric. Turn the piece right side out and press. Stuff each lightly and hand-stitch the openings closed. Work machine topstitching as indicated by the shorter dashed lines on the patterns.

2. Note: Refer to the photo below and diagram on page 91 for flower placement and stitching details. Assemble the appliqué center as follows: Arrange and pin all pieces onto the 22-1/2" square of velveteen, making sure pieces are at least 1" in from the edges. Tuck the iris petals under the iris center and fold them as shown. Place the tulip center under the tulip outer petal. Using matching threads, invisibly stitch each piece in place. For each four-petal flower center, cut a 2" circle of yellow fabric (there are no pattern pieces for the flower centers). Cut a 4-1/2" circle of gold for the rose center. Gather the circles, adding a small amount of stuffing, and stitch to the centers of the flowers.

3. Hand-embroider Outline Stitch stamens ending with French Knots. Scatter French Knots throughout the rose centers and tie knots of pearl cotton, leaving 1/2" ends around them. Machine-stitch meandering stem-like lines with green pearl cotton to indicate vines.

Strip-patch the Muslin Foundations

1. Prepare some of the fabrics following directions for Heirloom and other techniques in Part 2 (see page 129). Following instructions on page 89, Strip Patch the muslin foundations, adding laces into some of the seams. Work embroidery by hand and/or machine along patch seams and embellish as desired. Sew the shorter foundations to the sides of the floral center, then sew the longer pieces to the top and bottom.

Finishing the Quilt

1. With right sides together, sew on the satin borders. Work two rows of twining Outline Stitch along the inner seams in peach and rust pearl cotton.

2. Arrange the light green stem and leaves along borders as shown, pin, and slipstitch.

3. Shape the outermost edge of the satin border by carefully trimming it with shears into shallow curves, taking off only about 3/4" where the vine curves inwards. Press under 1/4" all around.

4. Place a dark green edging strip under the curved border at one side of the quilt. Keeping pieces flat and mak-

ing sure to have the width of a seam allowance underneath at inward curves, pin, then slipstitch. Repeat for the opposite edge and trim the ends even with the quilt. Slipstitch strips to the top and bottom of the quilt without trimming the ends.

5. Add the backing, wrong sides together, and baste. Turn the green edgings onto the backing, fold under 1/4", and slipstitch. Finish the corners neatly.

6. Cut the narrow ribbon

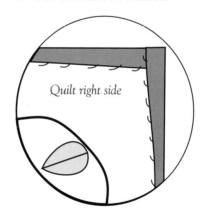

Quilt right side

into 10" lengths and tie them into bows. Tie the quilt by machine-tacking the bows onto the right side of the quilt throughout the Strip Patched areas. Hand-tie the floral center with matching pearl cotton, having the ties on the right side (see page 135).

Creative Notes

• There are many flower types that can be represented in stuffed appliqué. Observe flowers and try to approximate the shapes of petals and centers by cutting and sewing the shapes. Using the instructions above, make a stuffed appliqué quilt center using flowers you have designed.

Slender stems of six-foot-tall day lilies are highlighted against a blue and white sky.

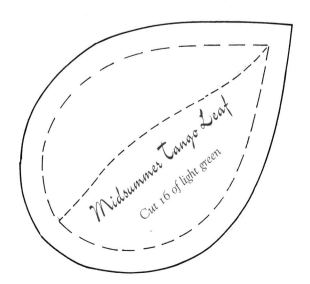

Midsummer Tango Leaf
Cut 16 of light green

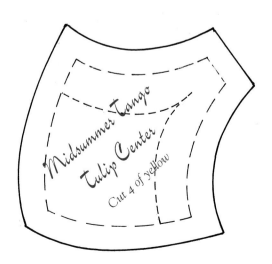

Midsummer Tango Tulip Center
Cut 4 of yellow

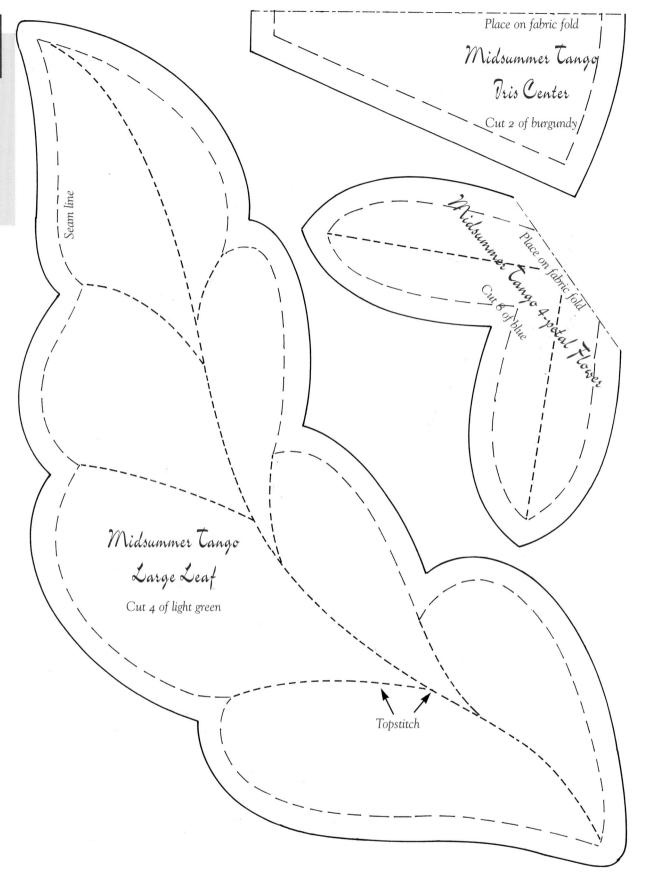

Place on fabric fold

Midsummer Tango

Iris Center

Cut 2 of burgundy

Midsummer Tango 4-petal Flower

Place on fabric fold

Cut 8 of blue

Seam line

Midsummer Tango

Large Leaf

Cut 4 of light green

Topstitch

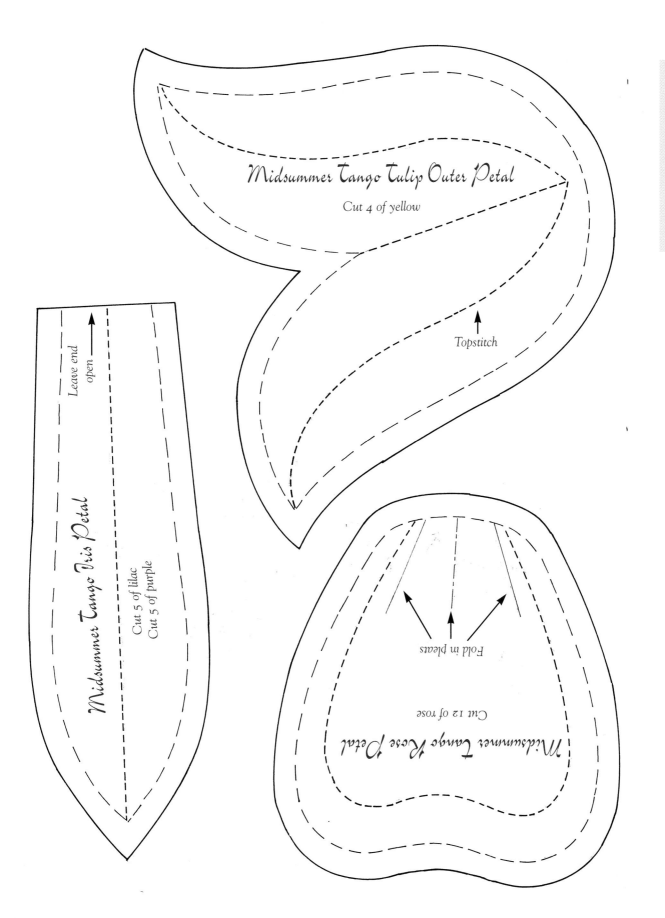

Midsummer Tango Tulip Outer Petal

Cut 4 of yellow

Topstitch

Leave end open →

Midsummer Tango Iris Petal

Cut 5 of lilac
Cut 5 of purple

Fold in pleats

Cut 12 of rose

Midsummer Tango Rose Petal

Pillow Quilt

The diamond-shaped "pillows" that compose this quilt provide an interesting edge treatment. The pillows are made individually, then joined at the seams. A pouffy bed-topper and attractive conversation piece, this quilt can be made to drape over the back of a sofa or to fit the top of a bed for a cozy comforter. The example shown here sports a Victorian color scheme enhanced by hand embroidery in lustrous rayon threads. (Machine Patch Seam Embroidery may be substituted, see page 122.) This is an excellent project for beginners.

Size: Individual diamond blocks are 5-3/4" x 7-1/2". (Make as many blocks as needed; for this type of quilt you can make and add blocks until it is the desired quilt size.)

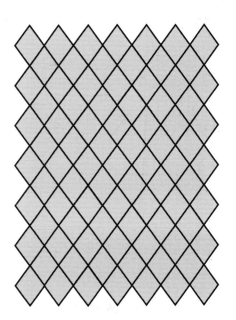

The Pillow Quilt is both cuddly and a conversation piece.

Palette

This quilt uses burgundy, gold, greens, cream, rose, peach, and the neutral colors taupe, brown, and silver patch colors, along with gold backing fabric, to form a Victorian-style color scheme.

Thread colors include fuchsia, bright yellow, dark green, gold, taupe, gray, black, white, and brown.

Materials

(This can be considered a "scrap" quilt to use up bits and pieces of fabrics and trims. Quantities will depend on the size of the finished quilt.)

- Scraps and small pieces of fabrics, including acetate satin; the cottons: sateen and velveteen; and cotton/rayon bengaline in the above colors
- Venice trims and cotton laces
- Muslin
- Cotton backing fabric in gold
- YLI Pearl Crown Rayon threads in the colors listed above
- Stuffing
- Size 8 pearl cotton to match the gold backing fabric

Note: Use 1/4" seam allowances throughout.

Cutting

1. Trace and cut out the Pillow Quilt Pattern.
2. Cut out the required number of shapes from muslin for your quilt size.
3. Cut out the same number of shapes from the backing fabric.

Making the Pillow Quilt

1. Following the instructions on page 89, Strip Patch the muslin using three to five fabrics on each and adding laces into and Venice trims along some of the seams.
2. Work hand embroidery along the patch seams using Pearl Crown Rayon (see Part 4).
3. Place a backing and a top right sides together and sew around, leaving an opening to turn. Trim seams, turn, and press.
4. Lightly stuff each pillow. (The quilt will be stiff if too much stuffing is used.)
5. Slipstitch the openings closed.

To Combine the Pillows

1. Sew the pillows together by hand using gold pearl cotton. Make several tiny stitches near the seam of the pillow to fasten the thread on. Holding two pillows with the backing sides together, stitch through the backing near the seam of one pillow, then through the other pillow, and repeat. Keep the stitches small and as invisible as possible. Fasten off with several tiny stitches.

Creative Notes

- Using photo transfer paper (following the manufacturer's instructions) and a photocopier, transfer black and white family photos onto the transfer paper, then iron them onto the fabric to use as some of the patches. Embellish the photos with lace and silk ribbon embroidery to make a quilt that will be a family conversation piece.
- This quilt also makes an interesting wall piece. Sew on a rod pocket and insert a dowel for hanging (see page 136).

This bouffant antique rose may well have been a Victorian garden favorite.

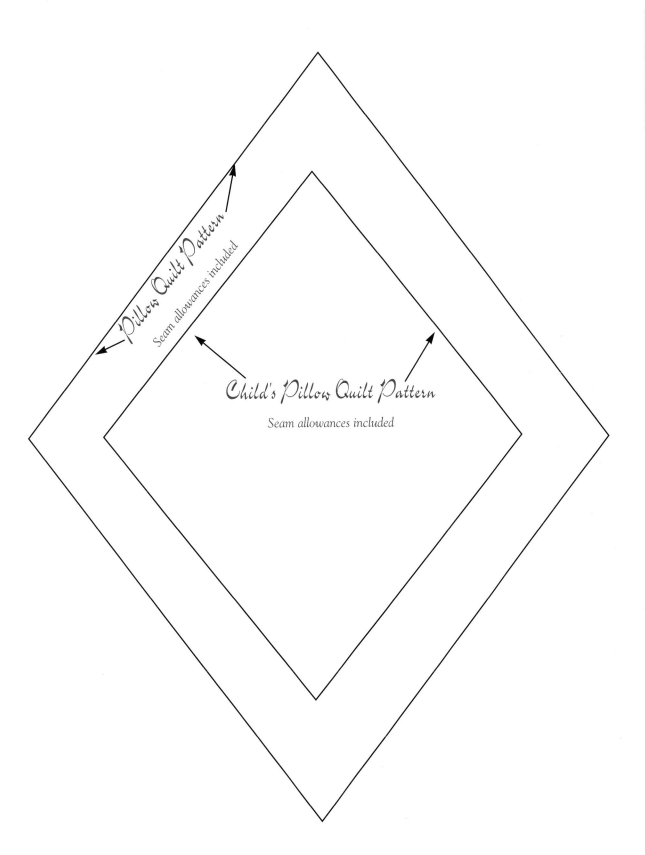

Pillow Quilt Pattern
Seam allowances included

Child's Pillow Quilt Pattern

Seam allowances included

Easy

Child's Pillow Quilt

For this version of the Pillow Quilt, use 100-percent cotton fabrics such as chintz, broadcloth, and sateen, white and ecru cotton eyelet laces, and size 8 pearl cotton for embroidery. To use as a crib quilt, stuff the pillows firmly and sew them together securely. Do not add anything that can be pulled off the quilt.

Size of blocks:
4" x 5".

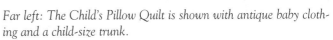

Far left: The Child's Pillow Quilt is shown with antique baby cloth-ing and a child-size trunk.
Left: The faces of pansies nod gracefully along the pathway.

Intermediate

Browns & Golds Strippie Quilt

A unique blend of old fashioned-looking browns and golds with flashes of silver lamé endow this quilt with an appearance both contemporary and of yesteryear. The dimensionality of trapunto and other surface work, along with soft velveteen fabrics and the warm colors, seems to portray coziness and warmth. Strip Patching is ideal for making large bed-size quilts because the individual strips are easy to handle and you simply make the number of strips needed for the desired quilt size.

Acetate lining fabrics figure prominently in this quilt. These fabrics are almost silky in appearance, easier to handle than silk, and are less prone to static. They are excellent for making shaped-edge, gathered, and tucked patches.

Size: 88" x 71" (eight 5-1/2" and seven 2" wide strips, 1" velveteen sashing, and 5-1/2" deep scalloped borders).

The machine-made Browns & Golds Strippie Quilt exhibits an old-fashioned air.

Palette

This quilt's color scheme is warm and rich, sparked by silvery accents. Use deep browns and black, adding antique and bright golds, cream, and silver tones. Bits of additional colors added as embroidery and embellishments include greens, red, and medium coral with mere touches of blue and purple.

Embroidery thread colors include rust, peach, jade, moss, pink, red, rose, burgundy, blue, and gray.

Materials

(All fabrics 44" wide)
- Scraps and small pieces of fabrics, including the cottons: velveteen and sateen; silver lamé with lightweight woven fusible interfacing ironed onto its back; and lightweight acetate lining fabrics
- 2 yards of brown velveteen (I used a soft print) for the quilt's sashings and upper edge
- 1/4 yard lengths of five or more colors of acetate lining fabric for the scallop borders

- 5 yards of muslin
- Venice and other laces, trims, wired ribbons, and silk ribbons for embellishments
- 5 yards of backing fabric
- Size 8 pearl cotton in the above colors
- YLI Quilting thread in 17 Peach
- Tracing paper, pencil, scissors

Note: Use 1/4" seam allowances throughout.

Cutting

1. Cut the muslin into 15 strips, eight 6" x 75-1/2" and seven 2-1/2" x 75-1/2".

2. Trace and cut out the border scallop pattern. Cut 30 scallops in assorted colors of acetate lining and 30 of muslin. Place one muslin piece on the back of each scallop and handle the two as one.

3. Cut the brown velveteen into one piece, 7" x 60-1/2", and two sashings, each 1-1/2" x 83" (piecing if necessary) and one bottom sashing 1-1/2" x 60-1/2".

4. Cut and sew the backing fabric into one piece, 89" x 72".

Making the Quilt Top

1. Prepare a quantity of patches using the methods in Part 2, including Through the Quilt Techniques (see page 124), Gathered Patches (see page 127), and Shaped-edge Patches (see page 127).

2. Strip Patch the wide foundation strips using mostly embellished patches. See Machine Embroidery techniques on page 122 to work machine Patch Seam Embroidery along patch seams and to use embellishments such as zigzag leaves and vines, medallions, trapunto, couched trims, and ribbons. See Ribbonwork on page 131 to add ribbonwork flowers and trims. Work machine and hand embroidery and silk ribbon embroidery as desired.

3. Strip Patch the narrow foundation strips without adding embellishments.

Finishing the Quilt

1. Sew the strips together, alternating wide with narrow. By hand, work a row of Herringbone Stitch (see page 140) along each seam.

2. Sew on the two side sashings, then sew the 7" x 60-1/2" piece of velveteen to the top of the quilt and the bottom sashing to the bottom of the quilt.

3. With right sides together, sew together eight border scallops, ending the stitching at the dots. Press the seams to one side and sew to the bottom edge of the quilt. Assemble eleven scallops for each side border and sew on.

4. Place the backing and quilt top right sides together and pin all around. Leaving an opening at the upper edge of the quilt, sew around the quilt, pivoting at the dots. Clip curves, turn, and press. Hand-sew the opening closed.

5. Machine-quilt in the pattern of your choice along the narrow sashings and the velveteen piece and topstitch along the scallops using the quilting thread.

Creative Notes

• Make a strippie tunic-vest by combining strips for the width of the back and half as many for each front panel. Sew the shoulders, then sew the sides up to the arm openings. Shape the front neck opening and sew in a knife-edge lining. (No pattern is needed, although you can refer to one for the neck and shoulder shaping if desired.)

Left: Brown and gray tones sometimes appear in the floral garden.
Above: Iceland Poppies are happy to fill in spaces between other plants.

Place on fabric fold

Browns & Gold Strippie Quilt
Border Scallop Pattern

Seam allowances included

Rhapsody in Silk

My goal for this quilt was to make a silk quilt entirely by machine. I really love to hand embroider with silks, and this was the hardest part—I almost had to sit on my hands at times to avoid adding hand work! Silk fabrics are truly a wonder. They are easy to dye in patch-size pieces in multitudes of shades and colors; with their drapey, near-weightless qualities, they are fabrics willing to defy gravity.

Due to the nature of silk, some prior experience in sewing lightweight fabrics is recommended before attempting a quilt-size silk project.

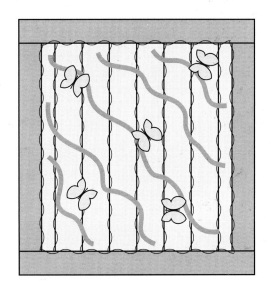

Size: 53-1/2" x 56" (5-1/4" wide borders). The size of the quilt is approximate due to the manner in which the foundation fabric is cut. See Prepare the Organza Foundations on page 112.

Rose petals cascade onto Rhapsody in Silk as the lady of the garden stands watch.

Palette

The muted colors in this quilt were inspired by a handful of Artemis' Hanah variegated bias silk ribbons. Picking up on some of the colors, I hand-dyed small pieces of silk fabrics and added some commercially-dyed pieces in compatible shades. Included are many earthy shades with blues and purples. The navy blue border sets off the colors in the quilt without distracting from them.

Materials

- 3 yards of 42" wide silk organza fabric in white or off-white
- Lightweight silk fabrics for patches in your choice of colors
- 1/4 yard lengths of several different white silk fabric types (such as jacquard, crepe, and satin) and Things Japanese Colorhue Instant Set silk dyes in the colors of your choice
- Assorted Artemis' Hanah bias silk ribbons
- Size 50 silk sewing thread, several spools in compatible colors
- Kreinik Soie Gobelin and Soie Perlee threads in assorted colors
- YLI size 30 silk thread in assorted colors
- Silk ribbons and other silk trimmings
- Silk batting (optional)
- 4-1/2 yards of silk border fabric such as dupionni or silk noil
- 3-1/2 yards of silk backing fabric
- Acid-free tissue paper
- YLI cotton Basting & Bobbin thread
- Tissue paper, pencil, and scissors

Note: Use 1/4" seam allowances throughout.

Hand-dyed silks can emulate shades such as those in this exotic-looking Iris.

Preparation

The preparation is a large part of this quilt.

1. Begin by dyeing silk fabrics and ribbons. Follow the manufacturer's instructions, mixing colors and adding water to obtain shades of your liking. Dry and press the silks.

2. Prepare patches, using silk threads and fabrics for the techniques in Creating Patches on pages 126 and 127. Make some patches with shaped edges, others with pintucks or pleats. Make organza sandwich and woven-ribbon patches. Also make five sets of organza sandwich butterfly wings. Work zigzag appliqués (see page 129) using your choice of subject matter. Couch silk threads and other fibers (see page 123). Use one or more layers of the acid-free tissue paper as a stabilizer for sewing some of the embellishments as needed.

3. Gather the edges of wide bias ribbons to use as patches. Instead of clean-finishing the raw bias edges, lightly fray them.

Yellow is purple's complement.

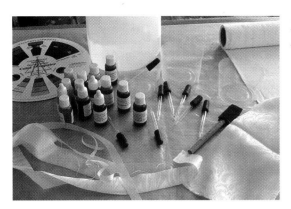

Dyes from Things Japanese are ready to be applied to silk fabrics and ribbons.

Butterfly Wings

1. To make butterfly wings like those shown in the photo, trace the wing pattern several times onto tissue paper.

2. Pin a tissue tracing to a completed organza sandwich (see page 126), straight-stitch along the drawn line, and remove the tissue paper.

3. Cut out the wing just outside the stitching.

4. Place the wing onto wash-away or iron-away stabilizer and zigzag or satin stitch entirely around the edges. Zigzag the interior lines.

5. Make a second wing using the drawn pattern upside down to reverse the wing. Sew the wings to the patched foundation with a 1/4" gap between them (see instruction 6 on page 113).

6. For the butterfly's body, tightly gather a 7mm silk ribbon and zigzag over it. Finish the ribbon ends by bringing them to the back using a chenille hand embroidery needle, or hand embroider the body.

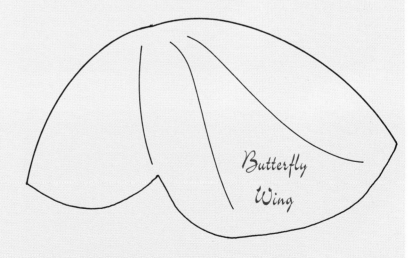

Butterfly
Wing

Prepare the Organza Foundations

1. Wash the organza to pre-shrink, press, and trim away the selvages. Cut a length about 46". Divide the width of the piece into six equal sections and carefully cut into six 46" long strips. Out of the remaining organza, cut and sew to make one additional strip the same size. Cut this strip down its length to make two equal narrow strips.

1. Cut and piece the tissue paper (fasten pieces together with hand-sewn basting stitches) to make strips the size of each organza foundation. Pin, then hand-baste, one to the back of each strip of organza. The tissue provides extra stabilizing for machine embellishments and prevents the organza from shifting during patching.

Patching and Finishing the Quilt

1. Following the instructions on page 89, Strip Patch the wide organza strips, using prepared patches and fabrics. Machine-straight stitch completely around each strip, staying inside the 1/4" seam allowance.

2. Machine-stitch the size 30 silk, Soie Gobelin, and Perlee threads in patterns along patch seams (see page 122). Add additional embellishments, such as couching heavier threads across the strips, sew-on trims, satin-stitch foliage, ribbonwork flowers and leaves, words and initials,

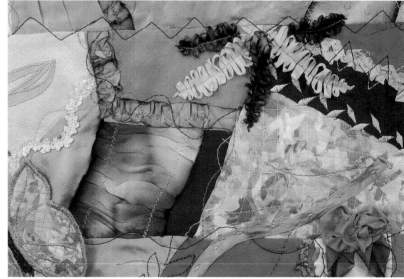

insets, and buttonholes with ribbons. See the Index in Part 2 for these and other techniques that can be used.

3. Strip Patch the narrow strips using silk fabric pieces with little or no embellishments. Edge-stitch as above.

4. Arrange the wide strips and sew them together, with right sides facing. Sew on a narrow strip to each side of the quilt top. Work machine Patch Seam Embroidery along the seams just sewn.

5. Cut bias strips about 1-1/2" wide out of any of the silk fabrics, fold in half lengthwise with right sides together, and sew into tubes using a 1/4" seam allowance. Turn the tubes right side out and press. Arrange them to meander diagonally across the quilt top as shown in the diagram and lightly baste in place. Sew buttonholes through the quilt (see page 125) to thread the tubes through. Remove the basting and replace the tubes through the buttonholes. Fasten in place by sewing the Dot Stitch (see page 124) along them.

6. Remove the tissue from the backs of the organza strips. Sew on organza sandwich butterflies, leaving the outer edge of each wing loose. Fabricated flowers (see page 132) may also be added.

7. Cut two borders from the dupionni or silk noil fabric, each 5-3/4" wide by the length of the quilt top, and sew one to each side. Cut a top and a bottom border, 5-3/4" wide by the total width of the quilt, and sew them on. Machine-sew meandering lines along the border seams in one of the size 30 silk threads.

8. Following the instructions in Part 3, add the batting, backing, and machine-tie the quilt. Make bias bindings out of the excess border fabric and bind the quilt.

Creative Notes

• Enjoy the process as you make a similar quilt without looking for an end result. You will see the piece transform on its own as more is added. Whatever creative choices you make will certainly individualize this quilt. Begin with colors you truly enjoy, prepare intriguing patches following most of the techniques given in Part 2, and just let it happen.

Day lilies are the subject of an appliqué.

Challenging

Victorian Elegance

Throughout this book, there are crazy quilts sectioned into blocks or strips, crazy quilting used as borders or sashings, and in combination with various techniques. This quilt is the grand finale— a geometry-based quilt which combines circle, square, rectangular, and fan shapes. The Victorian-style fans and wide crazy quilt borders make it a project not for the faint of heart. Assembly of the fans calls for precision sewing, and some prior experience in working with velveteen fabrics is recommended. Although hand embroidery is used in the quilt shown, machine embroidery and embellishments may be used instead.

Size: 65" square (35" square center and 15" x 30" Strip Patched panels).

Victorian Elegance framed by historical New england farmhouse architecture.

Palette

Here, jewel tones are combined with light and neutral colors. A rich, inviting burgundy gives this quilt a regal presence and Victorian feel.

Embroidery thread colors include burgundy, pink, violet, blue, gray, green, beige, peach, and black.

Materials

(All fabrics 44" wide)
- Scraps or small pieces of assorted fabrics, including 100-percent cottons: sateen, chintz, and velveteen; acetates such as satin and taffeta; and cotton/rayon bengaline in the colors listed above.
- 1/4 yard or larger pieces of cotton velveteen in assorted colors
- 1 yard of 100-percent cotton velveteen in burgundy
- 5 yards of muslin
- Several yards each of 1/2" wide braids, trims, and ribbons
- 5 yards of 1-1/2" wide leaf-pattern Venice cotton trim
- 7-1/2 yards of purchased or self-made binding
- 3-3/4 yards of backing fabric
- Size 50 100-percent cotton sewing thread in burgundy and colors matching the 1/2" wide trims
- Size 8 pearl cotton in light, medium, and dark shades of green
- Size 8 pearl cotton in the colors listed above
- Sew-on embellishments, such as photo transfers (see page 22), lace motifs, gimpes, silk ribbon for embroidery, ribbons for ribbonwork, and glass seed beads
- Tracing paper, pencil, and scissors

Note: Use 1/4" seam allowances for assembly.

Cutting

1. Cut one 36" square of burgundy velveteen and one of muslin. Place the muslin on the back of the velveteen and handle the two as one.

2. Out of muslin, cut eight 16" squares and four 16" x 36" border pieces.

3. Trace and cut out the fan pattern pieces. Cut pieces for six fans out of the velveteen fabrics.

Making the Quilt

1. Arrange and pin eight fan blades on each of six muslin squares (reserving two of the squares), keeping the excess muslin intact. Butt the raw edges of the fan blades up to each other, then use a wide machine zigzag exactly down the center of each butted seam so the stitches fall into two fan blades at once. Take care to keep the blades from shifting while sewing (you may need to pin or baste them first) and be sure the stitching adequately covers the raw edges.

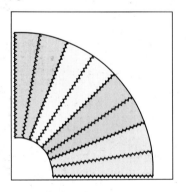

2. Lay a 1/2" wide trim onto each of the fans as follows: Cut the trims to the same lengths as the fan blades. Lay the 1/2" wide trim to cover a

zigzag seam and straight-stitch by machine along both edges of the trim to secure it. Sew two additional trims onto the outer edges of each fan. Hand-embroider a row of Single Feather Stitch along the edges of the trims.

3. Fold under and press the rounded edge of each fan center. Place one on each fan, overlapping 1/4" onto the blades, and pin. Add Venice trim to the folded edge and baste. Press under the lower edge of each fan header, place at the top of the fan, and pin. Baste the Venice trim to the folded edge. Embroider French Knots or sew on beads along the Venice trims to hold them in place. Trim away the excess muslin above the header.

4. Using one of the completed fan sections as a pattern, cut the two remaining muslin squares with a rounded edge to match. Following the instructions on page 89, Strip Patch the two muslins and the four border panels, adding laces and trims as desired. Embroider and embellish.

5. Combine and sew (with right sides facing) two of the fans and the two fan-shaped sections to make the circular center. Press seams and press the outer edge under. Center this onto the muslin-backed velveteen square, pin, and baste around. Slipstitch to the velveteen and muslin. Work Double Feather Stitch by hand along the slipstitched seam.

6. Carefully, taking care to not cut through the quilt, trim away the muslin and velveteen from behind the circular center, leaving about a 1/2" seam allowance (to eliminate the two extra layers of fabric). Save the cut-away fabrics for a future project.

7. Pressing seams to one side, sew a border section to each side of the velveteen center.

Sew a fan to each end of each remaining border panel. Sew one to the top of the quilt and the other to the bottom.

8. (See hand embroidery stitches in Part 4.) By hand, work meandering Outline Stitch along the seam around the velveteen square in medium green pearl cotton. Add Lazy Daisy "leaves" using dark green and work scattered French Knots in light green. Working freehand, embroider Outline Stitch branches at each corner in medium green. Add Single Feather Stitch "branches" in light green.

9. Following instructions in Part 3, add the backing and tie the quilt by machine and/ or by hand. Sew on a binding, adding sufficient ease at the rounded corners (otherwise the corners may bend inward or outward).

10. Make two velveteen "loops" to hang the quilt: Cut four pieces of velveteen, each 2-1/2" wide x 22" long. Place two right sides together and sew the long edges. Turn and press. Repeat for the remaining two pieces. Make a rod pocket (see page 136) and hang the quilt. Add the loops to the upper corners, looping them over the dowel, and pin and adjust until the quilt hangs properly. Hand-stitch the loops to the backing.

Creative Notes

• Sketch your own ideas for combining sections of various shapes like circles, fans, squares, and rectangles. See what geometric fantasy you can devise in the form of a quilt! Decide on how large to make your quilt, then cut the shapes the size you want out of newspaper. Lay them out on the floor or other surface. If the shapes are to your liking, cut them out of muslin to use as the foundations. When cutting muslin foundations and other pieces, be sure to add seam allowances.

Five-petal roses have as much charm and aroma as their many-petalled relatives.

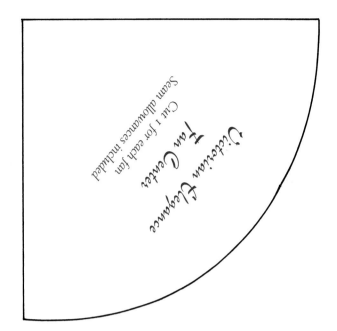

Victorian Elegance
Fan Center
Cut 1 for each fan
Seam allowances included

Victorian Elegance
Fan Blade

Cut 8 for each fan

Tape

Victorian Elegance Fan Blade

(Tape the pattern piece at the dotted line to complete the pattern.)

Tape

Victorian Elegance
Fan Header
Seam allowances included

Tape

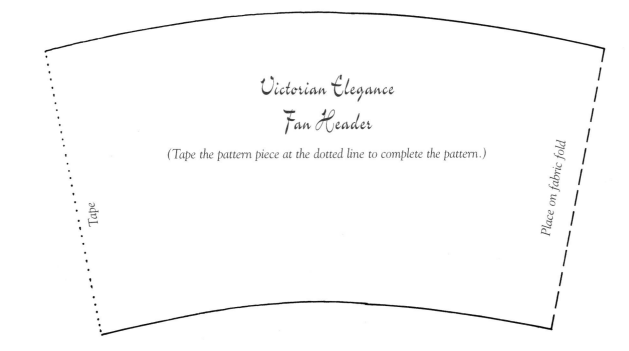

Victorian Elegance
Fan Header
(Tape the pattern piece at the dotted line to complete the pattern.)

Tape

Place on fabric fold

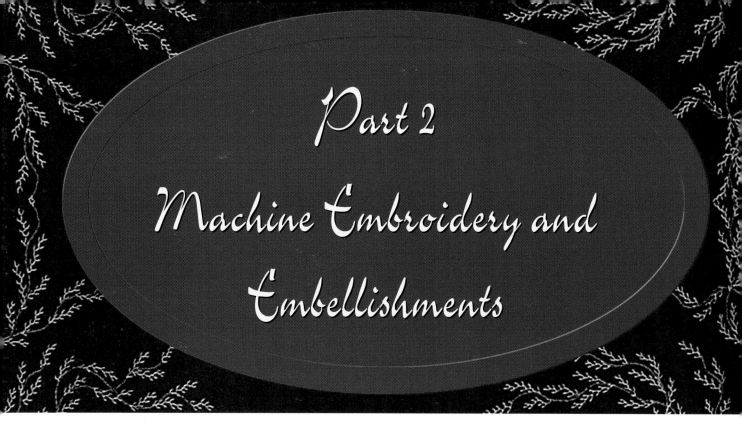

Part 2

Machine Embroidery and Embellishments

The following embroidery and embellishment techniques will add variety to your repertoire because they present quite a range of methodology. Some can be worked in lengths of fabric that are then cut up for patches, and others are intended for application after the quilt top is patched. Use them along with hand techniques as seen in many of the quilts in this book and covered in The Magic of Crazy Quilting, or try a quilt that is exclusively machine work.

Try each of the techniques given, explore the possibilities, and perhaps you will dream up some methods on your own!

Tools and Materials

Needles

Collect and try some of the many types and sizes of machine sewing needles available, including denim, metallic, quilting, topstitch, and embroidery. Experiment to find the ones that work best for the technique being done; I've found most to be somewhat interchangeable. There are different size ranges for the various types, with sizes running between 75/11 (small) to 110/18 (large) (in general for machine needles). I use the larger sizes with heavier threads and the smaller with finer threads. Pair metallic needles with metallic threads, topstitch or jeans needles with size 8 pearl cotton and other heavy threads, and the embroidery needles with size 40 and 50 silk, cotton, and rayon threads. Use a quilting needle for machine quilting through several layers of Confetti quilts.

In some of the instructions in this part, a size 18 chenille needle is called for. This is a hand-embroidery needle and is often used to bring the ends of the large threads and silk ribbons to the back for fastening off.

Stabilizers

Stabilizers make some embroidery and embellishment methods possible and others easier. A stabilizer is needed when machine stitching appears unevenly or distorts the fabric. Pin or baste the stabilizer to the back of the piece being sewn, sew through all layers, and remove it when finished. Those who use them tend to develop their preferences, so try the different types to find those that work best for you. Experiment with them using scraps of fabric. Some examples include:

Tear away: Take care not to pull stitches out of place when removing.

Tissue paper: Regular or acid-free (see typing paper). Use with lightweight fabrics such as silks.

Typing paper: Only use this where it can be completely torn away. In cases where bits of it are likely to remain, use acid-free paper.

Vanishing muslin (iron-away): A treated fabric that turns brown under an iron set on "wool," then can be flaked and pulled away.

Water soluble or (wash-away): Dissolves when water is applied.

The Tissue Paper Transfer Method

For transferring the outlines of embroidery designs, this method was introduced in *The Magic of Crazy Quilting*, but is equally useful for machine work.

1. Trace your design onto ordinary white tissue paper (the type used for wrapping gifts) using a pencil.

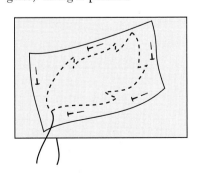

2. Pin the tissue to the fabric.

3. Machine stitch along the drawn lines.

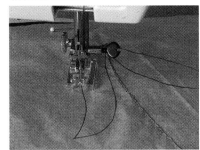

4. Tear away the tissue.

Tying off Ends

Bringing the ends of the top thread to the back and tying them off takes little time and is a necessity for a neat finish. If you simply cut the threads close to the fabric, you will soon have unsightly ends sticking up everywhere. Use this for all machine embroidery and embellishment techniques, except when sewing a very close zigzag (see Initials and Dates, page 123).

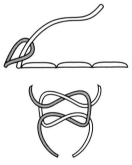

1. Turn the piece over so you are looking at the back of it. Take the bobbin thread and give it a tug; a small loop of the top thread will appear.

2. Insert the point of a seam ripper (or a needle), taking care to not cut the thread, and bring the top thread through to the back.

3. Tie a square knot and trim the ends to about 1/2" long.

Machine Embroidery

Collect some different thread types and experiment with them. Thirty and 40 weight cotton and rayon and size 50 silk threads are all wonderful for machine zigzag embroidery. Some heavy threads and metallics can be threaded into the machine for straight stitching, and other heavy threads can be couched. Use a stabilizer if needed (see the previous page).

For the bobbin thread, size 50 100-percent cotton sewing thread is good for most purposes like sewing with pearl cotton and couching. For fine zigzag and satin stitch embroidery, YLI's 100-percent cotton Basting & Bobbin thread works well.

The following are important for machine embroidery:

Feed dogs: Lower or cover for darning and use up for other methods.

Needle: (See information on page 120.) Because new needles work the best, change them on a regular basis.

Presser foot: Use an open or grooved foot for most embroidery. The foot must allow the stitching to pass underneath without hindrance. Decreasing the pressure on the foot (if your machine allows) makes it easier to manipulate the fabric. Check with your machine manual for specifics.

Stitch length: Use the longest for heavier threads, any width for finer threads, and set at zero for darning.

Stitch width: Various widths can be appropriate for couching and zigzag techniques and for decorative built-in machine stitches.

Tension: Turn the tension dial toward the lower numbers until the top thread begins to show through to the back. This allows the top thread to show up better and the bobbin thread to be less apparent.

Right: A selection of threads, machine feet, and needles used for machine embroidery.
Below: A thread stand allows pearl cotton to easily wind off of the spool.

Thread: There are many different threads available, and various types handle differently, so experiment!

Patch Seam Embroidery

Pearl cotton used in the sewing machine is a way to approximate hand stitching. Size 8 pearl cotton shows up well when sewn; however, if you cannot get it to work, use the finer size 12. Use regular cotton sewing thread in the bobbin with a dark thread for darker embroidery threads and light for lighter. Tie off the thread ends after each line of stitching (do not backstitch).

Place the spool of pearl cotton on a cone holder behind the machine, as shown in the photo, or wind it onto a bobbin so the thread can wind off unhindered. Any slight hindrance can cause the thread to snag the machine.

The diagram shows some patterns that can be sewn along patch seams.

Tips for success:
- Use a denim or topstitch needle.
- Decrease pressure on the presser foot.
- Use the longest stitch length.
- Stitch slowly.

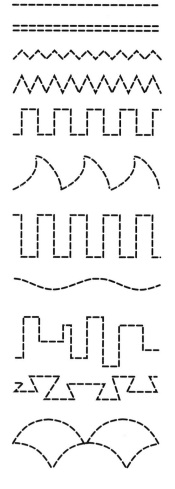

- Use typing paper as a stabilizer.

To make sharp turns, stop, lift the presser foot, turn the fabric, lower the foot, and proceed. Curved lines are done by gently turning the fabric while stitching slowly (easier if the pressure on the presser foot is decreased).

Add a second row to the first in a different thread color, or add hand embroidery.

Spiderwebs

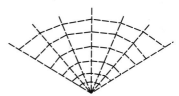

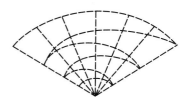

Spiderwebs are quick to make when stitched by machine. Experiment with various threads, including metallics and metallic blends, rayons, and silks. When using heavier threads, follow the instructions above for Patch Seam Embroidery.

1. Sew the straight lines of the web, tying the ends off after each line.

2. Sew the lines going across, either continuously or a line at a time.

3. Add a hand-embroidered spider (see the "Spider Stitch" in Part 4, page 141).

Couching

Couching is securing a thread, fiber, or trim in place by using a second thread to place stitches over it. By machine, zigzagging is commonly used.

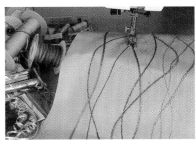

There are many materials that can be couched, including ribbons, rattail, soutache, heavy threads, yarns, and chenille. For efficiency, work couching over an entire quarter-yard piece of fabric, then cut off pieces as needed for crazy quilt patches.

Watch that the zigzag stitching is plunking down on both sides of the couching material, not into it. Create straight or curved lines, use interesting (matching or contrasting) threads in the machine, and try decorative or utility stitches if your machine has them.

Tips for success:
- Use a braid foot, embroidery foot, or a narrow hemmer. Feed the couching fiber into the hole of the braid foot, control it by hand with the embroidery foot, or guide it through the hemmer.
- For the top thread, use any that can be zigzagged, such as size 50 cotton or silk, rayon types, or a lightweight metallic like Kreinik's Cord.
- Use size 50 100-percent cotton sewing thread in the bobbin.
- Use a stabilizer if needed.
- Set the zigzag stitch width so it is slightly wider than the couching material.

Initials and Dates

Zigzag satin stitching by machine requires a very short stitch length. Adjust the length so the stitches fall immediately next to each other. The stitching can be gone over a second time if desired.

Your initials and the date of finishing the quilt make attractive embellishments. Use a size 50 cotton, silk, or a size 40 rayon thread.

This detail of the Browns & Golds Strippie Quilt (see page 105) shows zigzag embroidery and examples of trapunto and Slash & Pouf.

1. Draw the letter or number on the patch using a tailor's chalk pencil, or use the Tissue Paper Transfer Method (see page 121).

2. Begin and end each line of stitching with several stitches at zero length and width, then stitch at the desired zigzag width. Increase and decrease the width by moving the width dial or lever as you sew.

3. Trim the thread ends close to the fabric on the front, tug on the bobbin thread to bring the top thread to the back, and leave about an inch of bobbin thread hanging.

It will take some practice to smoothly sew curves and varying widths. Near-perfect results are possible, but a look of "done by hand" also has character.

Tips for success:
- Use an embroidery foot.
- Use a very short stitch length.
- Decrease the foot pressure for easier maneuvering of curves.
- Use plain cotton or YLI Basting & Bobbin thread in the bobbin.
- Use acid-free paper, wash away, or iron-away stabilizer.

The Dot Stitch

These little zigzaggings are a machine translation of French Knots. Use size 50 silk or cotton sewing thread, or rayon machine embroidery thread. Use any bobbin thread and an embroidery foot.

Rhapsody in Silk (see page 109) sports the Dot Stitch in addition to appliqué, couching, silk ribbon by machine, and a fabricated flower.

1. With the stitch length and width set at zero, make a few stitches in place, then stop and set the machine for 4mm or other desired width and a very short length.
2. Stitch until the stitches mound up (12 to 15 stitches), then set the stitch width to zero for several stitches.
3. Move forward to the next stitch placement, keeping the stranded thread taut between dots. Repeat, working a continuous row of dots.
4. To finish, trim all top threads close to the stitches. On the back, do not trim the threads or the stitches will fall out.

Medallions

These freeform stitching patterns are easy to create.

1. Put the fabric into an embroidery hoop, placing the fabric at the bottom of the hoop instead of the top. Thread the machine with any weight sewing thread.
2. Place the hoop under the needle and begin. Continuously make a looped and curved line, staying within a circular area to form a round medallion.
3. When the medallion is complete, remove the piece from the machine, bring the thread ends to the back, and tie.

Tips for success:
• Use a 6" to 8" embroidery hoop that will fit under the machine's needle.
• Drop or cover the feed dogs.
• Use a darning foot or no foot at all.
• Set the stitch length at zero.
• Practice steady movement of the hoop, running the machine slowly, and gradually increasing speed as you gain proficiency.

"Through the Quilt" Techniques

These techniques can be used after the quilt's patches have been sewn onto the foundation. The foundation acts as a stabilizer while providing an extra layer to enclose the stuffing used in trapunto.

Trapunto

Trapunto, which creates padded areas that add dimensionality to a quilt top, is very easy to do. Use regular sewing thread that either matches or contrasts with the fabric, depending on the look you want. (A good source of simple outlined designs is children's coloring books.)

The Browns & Golds Strippie quilt (see page 105) displays trapunto and other techniques.

1. Machine straight-stitch along the outlines of a design, but do not backstitch. Bring the thread ends to the back and tie off.

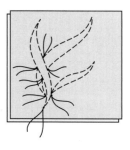

2. Very carefully, with sharp embroidery scissors or a seam ripper, cut a slash through the foundation only. Make the slash only as long as needed in order to add stuffing.

3. Use a blunt, pointed tool like a nail file to push in a tiny amount of stuffing. Stuff lightly.

4. To finish, thread a hand sewing needle and stitch together the edges of the slash.

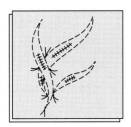

Slash & Pouf

This method adds a puffy piece of fabric into a patch. It seems a bit quirky, but is a way to add dimensionality.

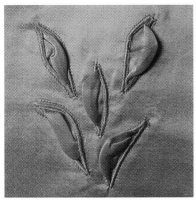

1. Machine-sew two side-by-side lines of close zigzag or satin stitch.

2. Using a seam ripper or sharp embroidery scissors, slash between the lines, but not all the way to the ends.

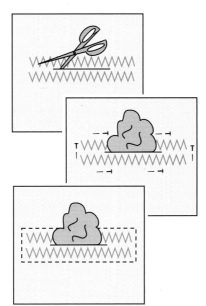

3. Take a scrap of fabric that is larger than the slash area, and, working from the back, push the center of it through the slash to the front of the crazy patch, creating a pouf. Spread the edges of the added fabric so it can be pinned on the front.

4. Straight stitch around the outer edges of the zigzagging to secure the added fabric in place.

Buttonholes

An ordinary thing like machine-made buttonholes can be used for decorative effects.

Buttonholes in Rhapsody in Silk (see page 111) accommodate meandering bias tubing. Also shown here are woven and organza sandwich patches.

1. Use your machine's buttonhole mechanism to make buttonholes the size of your preference.

2. Cut them open and draw ribbons through.

3. In the back, fasten the ribbons to the foundation with hand stitches.

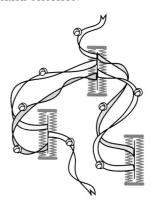

4. Hand-embroider French Knots or use the Dot Stitch (see page 124) along the ribbons on the front to fasten them in place.

Insets

Adding an inset is like creating a patch within a patch. Use the inset to highlight a lace motif or anything you'd like to place inside it.

A lace heart motif is nestled inside an inset on the Rambling Roses quilt (see page 21).

1. Place a second fabric over a crazy patch and stitch around in a circle or oval shape.

2. Inside the stitched lines, cut out the center, leaving a seam allowance of about 1/4". Clip to the seam allowance all around.

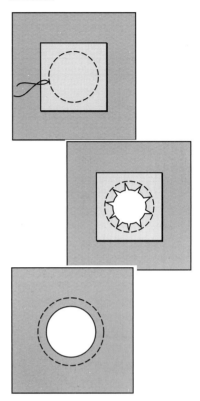

3. Push the added fabric inside the circle and to the back. Press the seam.

4. Place a fabric behind the opening and invisibly hand stitch it to the foundation. Topstitching may be worked around the opening. Add a lace motif or other embellishment to the new area.

Creating Patches

The following methods are creative ways to make patches that are then added into a quilt that is being patched. Accumulate a stack of created patches before beginning the quilt and use them for some of the patches.

Organza Sandwich

You will need pieces of silk organza fabric and trimmings of silk threads, ribbons, fabrics, and silk sewing thread for this method. Save all of your silk trimmings from embroidery and other silk projects. Even the smallest thread and fabric clippings and trimmings can be used.

1. Cut up the silk trimmings to make them really fine, or use them as they are. Place a thin layer onto a piece of silk organza fabric about 6" to 8" square.

2. Lay a second piece of organza on top and pin in several places.

3. Press, using a damp press cloth or steam.

4. Machine-quilt back and forth over the piece until it is well held together.

Weaving Ribbons

See the photo with Buttonholes on page 125 for an example of woven ribbons.

Begin with a piece of silk organza fabric, about 4" square. Lay 7mm silk ribbons onto it side-by-side in one direction. Pin, then sew along the ribbon ends to hold them in place. Weave additional ribbons through in the opposite direction until it is all filled in. Sew along the ends to secure; the piece can now

be quilted. Using silk thread, quilt lines either parallel or diagonal to the weaving, or use free motion quilting. Use the weaving as a patch.

Confetti Patches

The Confetti method in Part 1 (see page 57) can be used to create individual patches. Combine small pieces of a variety of fancy fabrics, then cut and sew them until the individual pieces are quite small. Also, keep your smaller cut-offs that usually occur during patching. Sew them together to create a patch.

Pleats

Pleats are simply folds made in fabric, which are then pressed or left loose. They can be partly sewn down, or sewn only across the ends. Pleat fabric pieces or scraps to use as individual patches, adding them to a crazy quilt the same as any patch. Start with a sizable piece of fabric because the pleats will reduce its total size.

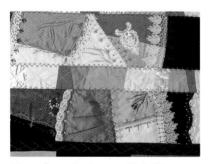

Pleats from the Brown & Golds Strippie Quilt (see page 105).

Three Ways to Make Pleats
1. Working across a patch, make a fold in the fabric, press, and repeat. Baste across both ends to retain the folds.

2. Pleat one end only and baste along that edge to retain the folds, allowing the opposite edge to remain flat.

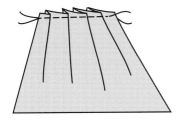

3. Pleat an already pleated patch, making the folds perpendicular to those already made.

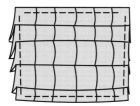

Gathered Tucks

Tucks are like pleats, but they are sewn into the fabric instead of being left loose. Again, allow extra fabric.

Here is a gathered tucked patch on the Browns & Golds Strippie quilt (see page 105), a spiderweb, and Slash & Pouf.

Wide tucks that are gathered seem to have a particularly Victorian look to them.

1. Fold a piece of fabric in two and sew about 1/2" from the fold using a long basting stitch.

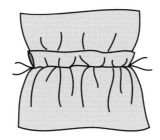

2. Pull on one of the threads from each end to lightly gather the seam, then tie the threads at both ends of the stitching.

3. Press to one side, flattening the gathers at the same time.

Gathered Patch

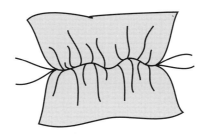

1. Sew across a patch using a long basting stitch.

2. Lightly gather by pulling one of the threads from both ends and tie the thread ends.

3. Press to flatten.

Variations on this theme can be done by sewing curved lines, or by sewing multiple rows and gathering each.

Shaped-edge Patches

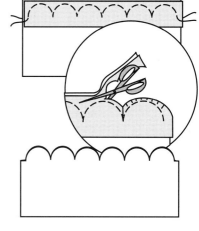

Choose a patch fabric and a second facing fabric about 3" to 4" wide and same length as the patch fabric. The two can be the same or contrasting. Lay them right sides together and edges aligned. Machine-stitch along this edge in a scalloped, wavy, or zigzagging line. Trim and clip the seam allowance. Turn right side out and press. After adding the patch to the quilt, add embellishments to the shaped edge to hold it in place on the quilt.

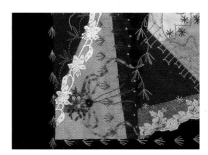

Machine Patch Seam Embroidery worked on the Rambling Roses quilt (see page 21).

Self-made Trims

Pipings, fringes, and ruffles can all be "store bought," but making them yourself means you can do them in the materials of your choice. Consider, for instance, using a fancy silk fabric for a piping or an exotic thread for a fringe.

Piping

1. Using a zipper foot, sew a strip of bias or straight-grain fabric over a core of cable cording or a bulky yarn.

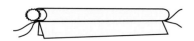

2. Sew with right sides together to the edge of a patch.

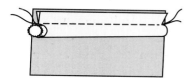

3. Press the seams to the back and topstitch in the ditch along the piping seam when sewing the patch to the quilt.

Fringe

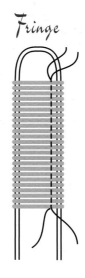

1. Bend a coat hanger into a "U" shape, wrap with thread or yarn, and stitch from one end to the other.

2. Cut along one edge and remove the fringe from the wire.

3. Topstitch it to a patch edge or sew it into a patch seam.

Ruffle

1. Machine-sew a close zigzag or satin stitch in a wavy pattern on a strip of fabric, then trim as near to the stitching as possible.

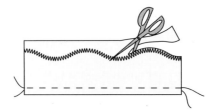

2. Gather along the raw edge.

3. Use the trim the same as eyelet lace, adding it into patch seams.

Appliqué

Appliqué is fastening one fabric onto another. It is often used to create shapes in the form of flowers or other objects. The following are three ways to machine appliqué.

Broderie Perse

Broderie Perse consists of cutting a motif from a piece of printed fabric which is then sewn onto a different background. Look for fabrics featuring bold florals and other designs that can be cut away from the background. Padding can be added by using the Trapunto technique (see page 124).

Broderie Perse decorates the Super Easy Blue Jeans Throw (see page 49).

1. Cut around the design to be used, leaving approximately 1/4" excess.

2. Lay the piece onto the background fabric and machine straight stitch around.

3. Trim the excess close to the stitching.

4. Sew a close zigzag or machine satin stitch to cover the previous stitching and the raw edge.

Sew 'n Turn

This method is used in the quilt Midsummer Tango (see page 91). The appliqués can be stuffed for dimensionality or left flat. It is a quick and easy appliqué method. Draw your shapes to size on paper to use as patterns.

1. Cut out the appliqué pieces, adding a 1/4" seam allowance. Cut two pieces for each part to be appliquéd. The second piece can be organza or bridal tulle for a thinner appliqué.

2. Hold the two pieces right sides together and sew completely around.

3. Cut a slash in the backing piece and turn right side out. Press. Add a pinch of stuffing if desired.

4. Slipstitch the appliqué to the background fabric right side up.

Zigzag Appliqué

This is creative appliqué. Once you understand how it works, it is possible (and easy) to cut freeform shapes out of fabric, sew them down, and add more shapes to the design, for instance layering flower petals and leaves, or placing a figure against a setting sun. Layers can be built up and new shapes continually added. It is easiest to learn

As shown on Rhapsody in Silk (see page 109), zigzag appliqué can be used for intricate shapes.

by beginning with a drawn design.

1. Draw the design on tissue paper, making one drawing per color, and stack them in the order they will be used in case there are background and foreground elements. Begin with the background.

2. Stack, beginning with the bottom layer: stabilizer, background fabric, appliqué fabric, and tissue drawing. Pin all layers.

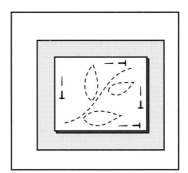

3. Using short machine stitches, sew along the outlines of the design.

4. Remove the tissue.

5. Trim the appliqué fabric very close to the stitching.

6. Sew a close zigzag to cover the lines. Use a narrow zigzag just wide enough to secure the appliqué if your shapes are small.

7. To add the following color, layer the appliqué fabric and then the tissue drawing, placing the drawing according to the design. Repeat for the remaining colors.

8. Add any embroidered details last, then remove the stabilizer.

Heirloom Sewing by Machine

Heirloom sewing consists of a group of techniques used mainly in the late 1800s and early 1900s for making exquisite garments for ladies and children, for example a high-necked Victorian blouse with lace insets, pintucks, soft ruffles, and gathered sleeves.

Heirloom methods can be used to make patches that are then added to a crazy quilt as it is patched. Experiment with other fabrics than the traditional semi-sheer batistes, lawns, and organdies, and with joining a variety of laces and trims. Use a matching thread, either a 100-percent cotton sewing thread, or the size 100 cotton thread made for heirloom work.

Pintucks

Check to see whether your machine has a specialty foot for twin-needle mock or regular pintucks. If so, set up the machine according to the manual and proceed to sew them.

Pintucks can be made on any machine by folding the fabric, creasing it, and stitching next to the fold. Unlike regular tucks, pintucks are narrow, about 1/8" wide or less. Press the tucks in either direction. Variations:
• Stitch across multiple pintucks to push them to one side or the other.
• Sew mock pintucks in curving and meandering lines across the fabric.

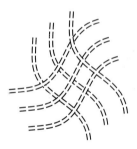

• Insert cording into a pintuck using a zipper foot.
• Pintuck a sheer fabric, lining it afterwards with a colorful fabric.

Entredeux

Entredeux resembles a tiny ladder with small square holes

Joining heirloom lace insertions by machine, Entredeux is simple to do.

in it. It is used to join two trims, or a trim to a fabric.

To Sew Entredeux to a Fabric

1. Place it right sides together with the fabric and machine straight stitch next to the edge of the ladder. Trim the seam allowances to about 1/8".

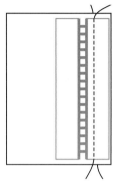

2. Cover the seam with a zigzag that covers the previous line of stitching and goes just off the trimmed edge of the seam allowance.

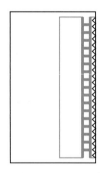

To Join Entredeux to the Finished Edge of a Ribbon or Lace

1. Trim off the batiste edge that will be joined.
2. Use a zigzag stitch, adjusting the width to have the needle plunk into each hole of the Entredeux, and just onto the edge of the trim. Have right sides facing up.

Two entredeux can be joined by aligning the holes and using a narrow zigzag that

goes into the next hole of each.

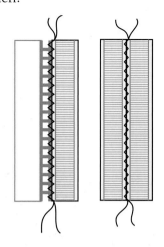

Also, ribbons or laces can be joined in much the same way, by butting them together, right sides up, and narrow zigzagging just onto the edges of each.

Heirloom trims are joined to form a patch in the Midsummer Tango quilt (see page 91).

Variations:
• Create an entire patch by joining entredeux, lace, and ribbons.
• Create a patch by joining ribbons.
• Slash a patch fabric down the middle and insert two rows of entredeux, a lace, a ribbon, lace again, then two rows of entredeux. Make several rows of pintucks in the fabric along each side of the insertions.

Ribbonwork

The dimensionality of ribbonwork florals gives them a presence that is eye-catching. Assemble flowers and leaves of various sizes into a motif. Add silk ribbon embroidery and some hand-embroidered feather stitch ferns to complete it.

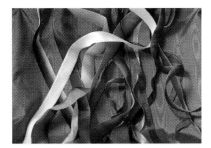

Collect a variety of quality fabric ribbons. My preference is for the soft and almost silky wired rayon ribbons that are made in France, some of which are in ombre colorings. There are also many beautiful silk ribbons in different widths, both satin and plain weave. If the ribbon is wired, remove the wire from the edge to be gathered, leaving the other wire to shape the flower.

Gathered Ribbon Flowers

Add these after the crazy quilt patching is completed. Use ribbons that are at least 1/2" wide to make small, delicate flowers and ribbons up to

Gathered ribbon flowers were sewn onto Midsummer Tango (see page 91).

about 1-1/2" wide for larger flowers.

1. Take a 12" length of ribbon and machine baste along one long edge.
2. Tie the threads at one end and machine tack this end to the quilt top. Pull on one of the threads to gather the ribbon and tie a knot close to the ribbon.

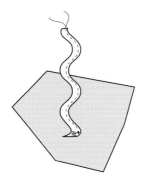

3. Use a hand sewing needle to bring the thread ends to the back.
4. Make several stitches through the flower to secure it, and fasten off.

Ribbon Leaves

This folded ribbon leaf is especially nice when added in bunches of two or three to Gathered Flowers above.

1. Using a ribbon about 1" wide or wider, fold twice as shown and stitch across to secure the folds. Trim away the excess ribbon below the stitching.

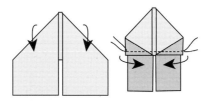

2. Gather the edge slightly and machine-tack to a patch.
3. Conceal the raw edge under a gathered ribbon flower.

Velveteen Leaves

Add these to Broderie Perse florals (see page 128) or to Fabricated Flowers (see below).

1. Take a small scrap of velveteen fabric and freehand zigzag satin stitch to create a leaf shape.
2. Cut it out next to the stitching.

3. Machine-baste along the center and gather slightly. Sew along the gathering line to fasten down.

Silk Ribbon Trimmings

Silk ribbons can be used to make pretty, delicate trims.

1. Using 7mm or wider silk ribbon, scrunch the ribbon under the presser foot while stitching it to a patch. Be careful of your fingers!
2. To make a loop trim of 4mm silk ribbon along a patch seam, begin stitching then stop, raise the foot, make a loop to the right, stitch it in place, make a loop to the left, and stitch.

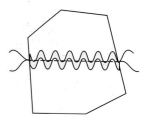

3. Continue making loops across the patch, then bring the ribbon ends to the back using a chenille needle.

4. Hand-embroider silk ribbon French Knots along the seam for decoration.

Ribbon Trimmings

Use fabric ribbons of any type such as silk, rayon, or satin to make these easy sew-on trimmings.

1. Gather both long edges of a 1" or wider ribbon. Meander it across a patch, machine straight stitching or zigzagging along the edges to fasten it.

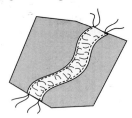

2. Machine-tack a tying length of ribbon to a patch. Tie a bow. The bow can be tacked down in places or left free.

Fabricated Flower

This makes a flower that is very dimensional. Use a lightweight fabric such as silk.

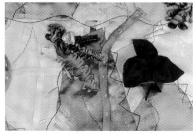

A burgundy fabricated flower and silk ribbon embroidery by machine are present on Rhapsody in Silk (see page 109).

1. Hold two 3" wide ribbons or two 6" to 8" lengths of silk fabric right sides together and, freehand, machine sew a wavy or zigzagging line similar to the diagram shown. Trim and clip the seam, turn right side out, and press.

2. Gather the lower edge.

3. Thread a hand sewing needle and begin to roll and scrunch the flower beginning at the narrow end. Tack and shape the flower as you roll, then hand-tack the flower to the quilt top along with several ribbon leaves. Bring the outer petals down and tack in place to conceal the raw edges.

Silk Ribbon Embroidery by Machine

Here are a fern and a rose for simple straight stitching by machine directly onto a crazy patch. Silk ribbon embroidery by machine can also be done by setting the machine for darning and using darning stitches to form the ribbons into various shapes. Experiment with both ways to dream up stitches and flowers.

A plain line of stitching secures silk ribbon formed into loops.

Use silk ribbons that are 2mm, 4mm, and/or 7mm wide. Thread the machine with matching size 50 silk sewing thread and use regular cotton sewing thread in the bobbin. Use a very short machine stitch length and an embroidery foot.

Leave about 4" of ribbon at each end of the stitching. To fasten off, thread an end into a size 18 chenille needle and bring it to the back. Work it into the foundation fabric with one or two small stitches.

Fern

Ferns are easier to make if the pressure on the presser foot is decreased. Use an embroidery foot.

1. Beginning at the top of the fern, plunk the needle into the ribbon to hold it in place and lower the presser foot.

2. Take hold of the ribbon and slide it under the foot and off to one side to create a small loop. Stitch over the ribbon, then make another loop in the opposite direction and stitch over it.

3. Continue, making each loop increasingly larger until the fern is the desired size.

Rose

1. Leaving a 4" tail at both ends, wind silk ribbon around your index finger tip 12 to 14 times.

2. Taking care to retain the coils, slide it off your finger and place on a patch.

3. Stitch across the rose, then bring the ribbon ends to the back. The coils will fluff up to obscure the stitching.

Part 3

Finishing the Quilt

The following consists of guidelines for finishing your quilt. Read through the section to find the information needed. There are often different ways to go about the final stages of assembling a quilt, and you can choose the way that is best or easiest for you. For instance, the knife-edge provides a clean finish without the need for bindings, and there are several ways to tie a quilt. Some information on how to care for a finished quilt is also included.

Assembling Blocks into the Quilt Top

To assemble a quilt made of blocks, first lay out the blocks on a clean floor and arrange them as desired. Then, sew them into vertical columns, adding spacers if they are indicated. Using a press cloth, press the seams to one side. If embroidery is to be worked along the seams just sewn, it is easiest to do it now rather than after the whole top is assembled.

Sew the first two columns together, adding a sashing if

indicated, and press the seam(s). Work any embroidery along the seam. Add the next column, press, and embroider. Continue until the quilt top is assembled.

Note: Work embroidery along the seams carefully, because it is partly intended to hold the seam allowances flat.

Adding Borders

For quilts consisting of patches placed onto a foundation, the extra layer of foundation should be repeated in all added parts such as borders and sashings as indicated in

the instructions for each quilt. This makes the quilt top consistent in weight and thickness; however, where a heavier fabric such as cotton velveteen is used, there is no need for a muslin interlining.

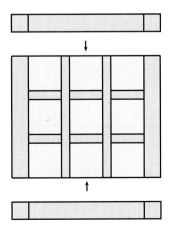

Sew on the two side borders and press the seams toward the borders. Sew on the top and the bottom borders and press the seams.

Battings

Battings are added to some, but not all, of the quilts in this book. Cotton battings that can be tied up to 8" to 10" apart are excellent, although polyester battings may also be used. A layer of cotton flannel fabric can be substituted for batting. If you are making an all-silk quilt, a silk batting should be used.

Backing

Suitable fabrics for quilt backings include smooth 100-percent cottons such as broadcloth, sheeting, sateen, and lightweight twill. Printed quilting cottons may also be used.

An all-silk quilt that has a silk batting should also have a silk backing for the sake of continuity and to keep the silk batting in place (silk clings to silk). Choose a medium-weight woven silk.

If the quilt is wider than the yardage, purchase twice the length of the quilt (three times if the quilt is very wide), plus extra to allow for seams and shrinkage.

Prewash the fabric and trim off the selvages. Make seams as necessary to make the backing the same size as the quilt.

Attaching the Backing

There are two ways of attaching the backing referred to in the instructions for the quilts in this book: knife-edge and the use of binding.

Knife-edge

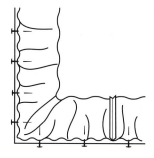

This type of finish gives a clean edge with no need for a binding.

Place the backing right sides together with the quilt top and machine-sew around, leaving an opening large enough to turn the quilt right side out. Trim the corners, turn the quilt, and press. Slipstitch the opening closed.

You may add gathered lace into the seam before it is sewn. Pin this to the quilt top, adding extra gathers at the quilt's corners (otherwise they will appear constricted afterwards). Hem the short ends of the lace, then add the backing and sew as above.

Binding the Quilt Edges

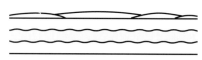

1. Place the backing right side down on a clean floor, then add the batting (if used), and lay the quilt top on top, right side up. Arrange smoothly in layers, in perfect alignment. If the quilt is be tied, see the instructions below, but if it is to be machine quilted, baste, then complete the machine quilting. To baste for machine quilting, make running stitches about 2" to 3" long through all layers diagonally, horizontally, and vertically. Begin all

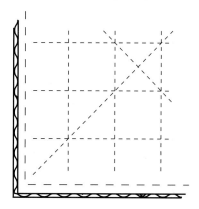

basting from the center of the quilt and work outward.

2. Baste around the outer edge. If a batting is used, trim it evenly with the quilt edges.

3. Purchase a 1/2" wide double-folded bias tape, or make a bias or straight-grain binding (instructions follow). Open out the binding and sew it with right sides together to opposite sides of the quilt. Trim even with the quilt at each end. Fold the binding to the back of the quilt, pin, and slipstitch. Attach bindings to the top and bottom of the quilt in the same way, but make the bindings 1/2" longer than the quilt at both ends. Clean-finish the binding ends by folding in neatly and slipstitching in place.

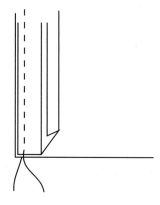

Make Your Own Binding

To Make a Bias Binding

1. Begin with a piece of fabric 36" square. Fold the fabric diagonally and press along the fold.

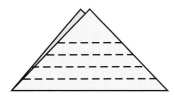

2. Cut along the crease, then proceed to cut sufficient strips of the required width to make up the needed yardage. Use a rotary cutter, acrylic ruler, and a cutting mat.

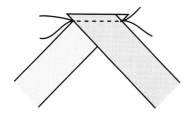

3. Sew the strips together, pressing the seams open or to one side. To make 1/2" wide finished bias binding, cut 1-1/2" wide strips and sew to the quilt using 1/4" seam allowances. (If you are using 1/2" seam allowances, cut the strips 2" wide.)

To make a straight-grain binding, cut along the width or length of the yardage to make strips the length and width needed.

Tying a Quilt

If the quilt is to have a batting, purchase one that can be tied 6" to 8" apart.

1. Lay the quilt on a clean floor or large table, and check that the layers are spread evenly throughout.

2. Baste through all layers, or pin-baste (use quilter's safety pins) to keep the layers from shifting.

3. Thread a hand sewing needle with a doubled strand of pearl cotton.
Starting anywhere (if the quilt is large, you can start at one end, rolling the quilt as you proceed), make a short stitch through all layers, pull through, and cut, leaving the ends long enough to tie.

4. Tie a square knot and trim the ends to about 1/2" long.

5. You can also make a series of stitches, then cut the thread between them and tie at each stitch. (The ties can be made to tie either on the front or the back of the quilt.)

Machine Methods of Tying a Quilt

Methods 2 through 4 add embellishments to the face of the quilt.

1. Using regular sewing thread, sew tacking stitches "in the ditch" or in areas they won't show. Bring the thread ends to the back, tie and thread them into a hand sewing needle, and bring them inside the quilt's layers.

2. Make ribbon ties: Take 10" of 1/8" wide grosgrain ribbon and tie into a bow. Machine-tack the bow to the quilt. Purchase several yards; you will get 3-1/2 bows per yard.

3. Sew on buttons by machine. First, check with your manual to see whether your machine has the appropriate foot for this.

4. Make the Dot Stitch by machine (see page 124), tying the ends of each dot on the back of the quilt and finishing thread ends as in Method 1 above.

Machine Quilting

Use a thread made for quilting, such as YLI's Quilting Thread, for the top thread and use a plain cotton thread to match the backing fabric or monofilament thread in the bobbin.

1. With the quilt right side up, use a walking foot to have the layers feed through the machine evenly.

2. Leave thread ends at both ends of each line of stitching and finish them off before they get tangled in with other lines of stitching.

3. To work in the ends on the back of the quilt, tug on the bobbin thread to bring up a loop of the top thread. Slide a hand sewing needle through the loop and pull up on the needle to bring the thread through. Tie a square knot.

4. Thread the ends into the sewing needle, then bring the needle into the backing and up about 1" away. Tug on the ends to sink the knot. Trim close to the quilt surface.

Stitch in the Ditch

Use a regular machine foot and cotton thread on top and a matching or filament thread in the bobbin. Stitch exactly on top of the seams of the piecing and finish the thread ends as above.

Slipstitching

Slipstitching is used for attaching a folded edge to another fabric, for instance, appliqués and bindings. Use a small needle, a size 12 "sharp," and 100-percent cotton sewing thread. Thread the needle and either make a knot in the end, or take a few tiny stitches in the fabric to secure the end. Run the thread over beeswax to help prevent tangles.

Slide the needle into the fold, making a small stitch. In the same movement, catch the second fabric with a very tiny stitch, which usually consists of only a few threads of the fabric. Repeat. The finished stitching should barely show, if at all.

Rod Pocket

Hem the short ends of a 6" to 8" wide strip of fabric that is the same length as the width of the quilt. Turn in the long edges 1/4" and press and slipstitch to the top of the quilt backing. A rod pocket can also be made as a tube to protect the quilt's backing.

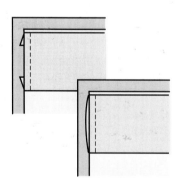

Cut the strip twice as wide as above, sew into a tube, and slipstitch to the quilt. A dowel is placed through the rod pocket for hanging the quilt.

Cleaning and Storing Finished Crazy Quilts

You can wash quilts that have washable, colorfast materials and if its fabrics have been prewashed. Wash your quilt in a large tub by soaking it in cool water and mild soap. Use a non-detergent unscented soap or one specifically for quilts. Do not agitate or wring. Allow the soap to be pulled out of the fibers by draining the tub. Refill with water, soak, drain again, and repeat this until the water runs clear. Do not pick up a waterlogged quilt. Carefully press out most of the water, then blot the quilt with towels. Drape it over a drying rack or several lines and dry away from sun and heat. Drying outdoors in the shade on a dry, breezy day is ideal.

Fancy crazy quilts, especially those with handwork, should not be washed, but lightly vacuumed only, using netting over the nozzle of the hose, and light suction to remove fine dust particles. Do this on a regular basis so that dust does not accumulate.

To store quilts, they may be wrapped in old, clean cotton sheets or acid-free tissue paper. Store them out of contact with wood, cardboard, or plastic. An armoire or trunk kept away from water, heat, dust, etc. is ideal. You can add sachets of potpourri that is meant to keep bugs away. Get the quilts out for refolding on a regular basis, preferably several times each year.

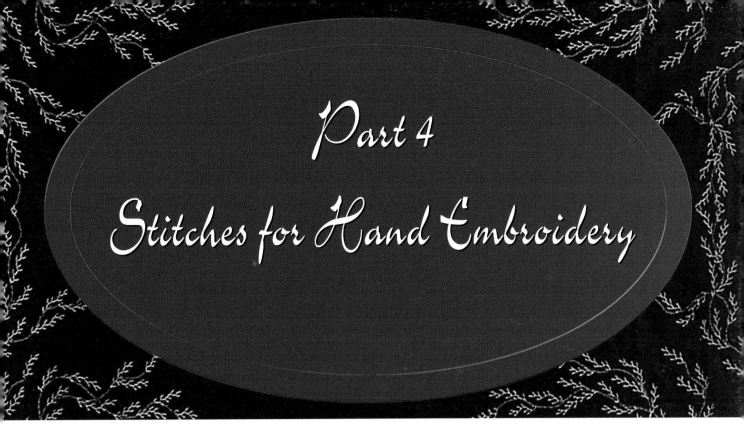

Part 4
Stitches for Hand Embroidery

In Victorian crazy quilts, hand embroidery was used to hold the patches in place (they were not machine or hand sewn). Here are a few of the many stitches that can be used along patch seams. Use embroidery stitches by themselves or add them to machine embroidery and embellishment methods. For placement ideas, refer to the photos throughout the book.

Note: To work silk ribbon embroidery by hand, my book *Ribbon Embroidery, 178 Iron-on Transfers* (Dover Publications, 1997) gives complete instructions and iron-on patterns (see Further Reading). The same stitches given below can be used for silk ribbon embroidery.

Materials

- Embroidery/crewel needles in assorted sizes
- Embroidery hoop, if needed
- Embroidery scissors

Recommended Threads for Crazy Quilt Seam Embroidery

- Soie Perlee, a twisted silk
- Pearl Crown Rayon, a twisted rayon thread
- Size 8 Pearl Cotton

• Fasten thread on and off by taking several tiny stitches close together through the foundation.

• Perfectly even stitches are not essential.

• Suggestions for combining stitches include using either Buttonhole, Cretan, Feather, or other row stitches for a base row, then adding French Knots, Lazy Daisy, Star, and other singular stitches to it.

• Use an embroidery hoop if your stitches tend to "bunch" the fabric.

Stitches for Hand Embroidery

The following are some basic embroidery stitches commonly used along crazy quilt patch seams. For more on hand embroidery stitches for crazy quilting, refer to *The Magic of Crazy Quilting*.

Note: The stitch diagrams that may be difficult for left-handed stitchers to follow are shown mirrored.

Blanket Stitch

When the stitches are made very close together, this is called the Buttonhole Stitch.

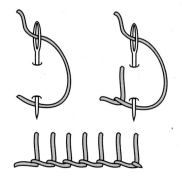

1. Make a vertical stitch with the thread under the needle. Pull through.

2. Make a second stitch to the right of the first, then continue.

3. Finish with a short tacking stitch. This stitch can be worked toward the right or the left.

Detached Buttonhole Stitch

This stitch is wonderful for adding tiny leaves to floral embroideries.

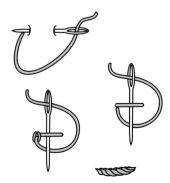

1. Make a Straight Stitch, bringing the needle up at one end of it.

2. Without piercing the fabric, work Buttonhole Stitch along the Straight Stitch.

Bullion Stitch

This stitch may take a few tries to learn, but afterward is easy to do and makes a wonderfully dimensional stitch. Form a bumblebee by alternating rows of yellow and black Bullion Stitch, adding French Knots for eyes and Lazy Daisy for wings.

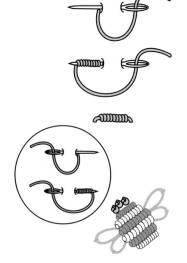

1. Begin making a stitch but do not pull through.

2. Wrap the thread evenly around the tip of the needle as shown, then carefully pull the needle all the way through while holding the wraps in place. Tug a little to even up the wraps.

3. Bring the needle down at the beginning of the stitch.

Cretan Stitch

Very quick and easy to do, the Cretan is a wonderful base-row stitch. Decorate it with French Knots or Lazy Daisy stitches.

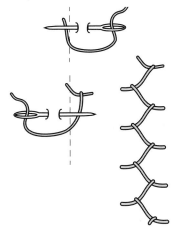

1. With the needle held horizontally, first take a stitch at one side, then the other of an imaginary line, working downward.

2. End with a short tacking stitch.

Feather Stitch

Work the Feather Stitch along seams and to indicate fern-like foliage.

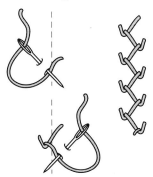

1. Working downward, make a short slanting stitch first to the left, then to the right of an imaginary line.

2. End the row with a short tacking stitch.

Double Feather Stitch

For this stitch, begin the same way as the Feather Stitch, but make an extra stitch to each side.

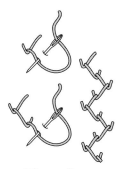

Fern Stitch

To achieve the Fern Stitch, make a vertical Straight Stitch, then work a series of Fly Stitches beneath it.

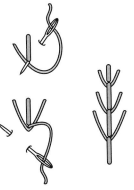

Fly Stitch

1. Make a stitch as shown, pull through, then fasten with a tacking stitch.

French Knot

A versatile stitch, French Knots can be used for flower centers. Scatter them across patches and along patch seam embroidery.

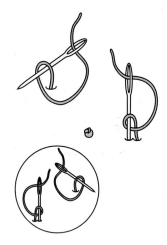

1. Wrap the thread around the needle, following the direction shown.

2. Pull snug, then bring the needle through to the back near to where it first came through.

3. Vary the stitch by wrapping two, three, or four times, making the knots loosely.

Pistil Stitch

1. Make these the same way as the French Knot, but sink the needle farther from where it first came through.

Herringbone Stitch

This stitch is quick to do once learned.

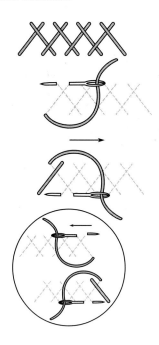

1. Following the diagrams, first make a stitch at the top, then the bottom of the row, moving toward the right.

Lazy Daisy

Make these individually to accent previous stitching or in groups for flower petals.

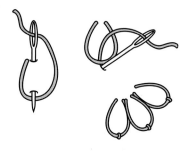

1. Make a stitch, having the thread go under the needle. Pull through.

2. Fasten the loop with a short tacking stitch.

Outline Stitch

Stitches for Outline Stitch can be made close together, or farther apart, in lines that are curved or straight.

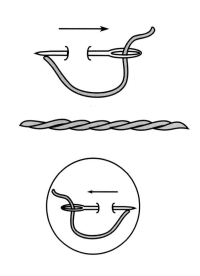

1. Keeping the thread below the needle, work toward the right.

Running Stitch

Made very small, this is the hand-quilting stitch. With stitches made longer, it is used for basting or embroidery.

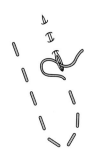

1. Make stitches evenly along a straight or curved line.

Star Stitch

These make delightful accents along rows of previously made stitching.

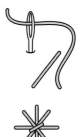

1. Make a cross stitch of two slanting stitches.
2. Make a second cross over the first with a vertical and a horizontal stitch.
3. The stitch can be "tied" in the center with a short tacking stitch.

Straight Stitch

Make them any length, in any direction. Group them to form fans and flowers.
1. Simply make a stitch from one point to another.

My Inventions

Here are a few of my own stitch inventions, made from varying or combining the stitches shown previously. Try coming up with some unique stitch inventions of your own!

Bird Tracks

This is kind of a free-form Cretan Stitch, an example of how stitches can be creatively transformed in the process of making them. Add several extra stitches at each side of the stitch.

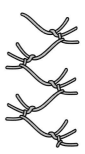

Fly n' Saucer

Work a Fly Stitch, then make a sideways Lazy Daisy on top of it. This looks like an acorn, or, if you make the stitches wide, a flying saucer.

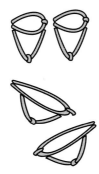

Spider Stitch

This is a grouping of stitches made in the form of a spider. I try to embroider at least one on each of my fancy quilts.

Combine Star Stitch, several Bullion stitches, add French Knots for the eyes, and then make Straight Stitch legs.

Sizes for Bed Quilts

The following are standard sizes for mattress tops. You will need to measure your mattress plus the amount of drop desired. For the drop, add the required amount to both sides and the lower end. Also decide whether extra should be added at the top if the quilt will be covering pillows. Quilts are often made as coverlets reaching to the top of a dust ruffle.

Crib mattress:
27" x 50"
Twin bed mattress:
39" x 75"
Double bed mattress:
54" x 75"
Queen bed mattress:
60" x 80"
King bed mattress:
72" x 80"

Further Reading

Duncan, Marie and Betty Farrell. *Ribbon Embroidery by Machine*. Iola, Wisconsin: Krause Publications, 1996.
*Demonstrates the darning technique.

Eddy, Ellen Anne. *Thread Magic, The Enchanted World of Ellen Anne Eddy*. Bothell, WA: Fiber Studio Press (The Patchwork Place), 1997.
*The works of an advanced machine quilting and embroidery artist.

Fanning, Robbie and Tony. *The Complete Book of Machine Embroidery*. Iola, Wisconsin: Krause Publications, 1980.
*Gives detailed information about machine settings, techniques, etc.

Fanning, Robbie (foreword). *Singer Instructions for Art Embroidery and Lace Work*. Menlo Park, CA: Open Chain Publishing, 1989. Reprint from 1941.
*A fascinating resource for what can be done with a straight-stitch-only sewing machine.

Kling, Candace. *The Artful Ribbon*. Lafayette, CA: C&T Publishing, 1996.
*Hand techniques and many ideas for combining ribbons into motifs; has antique examples.

Lehmen, Libby. *Threadplay, Mastering Machine Embroidery Techniques*. Bothell, WA: That Patchwork Place, 1997.
*Covers all facets of machine embroidery, including threads, tools, techniques, and quilt finishing

McGehee, Linda F. *Texture with Textiles*. Shreveport, LA: Ghee's, 1991.
-- *More… Texture with Textiles*. Shreveport, LA: Ghee's, 1993.
*Creating textured fabrics that could be used for crazy quilting.

Michler, J. Marsha. *The Magic of Crazy Quilting, A Complete Resource for Embellished Quilting*. Iola, Wisconsin: Krause Publications, 1998.
*Complete embroidery stitch instructions, 1,000 stitch variations, hand embellishments, and color photos of contemporary and antique crazy quilts.

--*Ribbon Embroidery, 178 Iron-on Transfers*. Mineola, NY: Dover Publications, Inc., 1997.
*Instructions for silk ribbon embroidery and motifs suitable for crazy quilts.

--*Shadow Work Embroidery, With 108 Iron-on Transfer Patterns*. Mineola, NY: Dover Publications, 1999.
*Motifs can be used for other types of embroidery; shadow work can be used for crazy patches.

Noble, Maurine and Elizabeth Hendricks. *Machine Quilting with Decorative Threads*. That Patchwork Place (Martingale & Co.), 1998.
*How to use many of the thread varieties that are available.

Pullen, Ph.D., Martha Campbell. *Antique Clothing, French Sewing by Machine*. Huntsville, AL: Martha Pullen Company, Inc., 1990.
*Techniques for heirloom sewing with many gorgeous examples.

Wolff, Collette. *The Art of Manipulating Fabric*. Iola, Wisconsin: Krause Publications, 1996.
*Highly recommended for designing your own textured patches.

The motifs on this page were used for trapunto (see page 124) in the Bullions & Battenberg Wool Quilt. They may also be used for appliqué (see page 129). Transfer them by using the Tissue Paper Transfer Method on page 121.